Striptease

Stripping For Beginners

by
Brenda Henning

Bear Paw Productions

4015 Iona Circle • Anchorage, AK 99507

(907) 349-7873 • Phone & FAX

Dedication

This book is dedicated to my children, Beth, Christi and Joshua ~ the reason that my quilt construction must be speedy. Every moment spent away from them is an opportunity missed forever.

Acknowledgements

I must thank my students, who, throughout the year, serve as my guinea pigs as I test the patterns in class. Thank you - you know who you are!

Credits

Written and illustrated by Brenda Henning.
Edited by Marcia Harmening.
Photography by:
　Ken Wagner
　1100 East Union
　Seattle, WA 98122
　(206) 328-1030
Machine quilting by Norma Kindred.
Printed in the United States of America.

ISBN 0-9648878-7-8

Striptease ~ Stripping For Beginners©
© 1999 by Brenda Henning
Bear Paw Productions
4015 Iona Circle
Anchorage, AK 99507
(907) 349-7873

Introduction

In the quest for speedier quilt top construction, some wonderful woman created the idea of sewing strips of fabric together and cutting those sewn strips into smaller pieces - eliminating many, many little squares, rectangles or diamonds. Not to mention the many hours normally spent marking, cutting and sewing those little pieces together. I personally would like to shake her hand.

I expect this revelation came in the middle of the night. Quilters do not spend much time sleeping. And when we sleep, the sleep is more a twilight type of sleep that allows continued quilt construction while dreaming. Why would we want to waste that valuable time in a nonproductive dreamland?

The strip pieced method of quilt construction is a relatively new development in quilt making. In the recent past, entire quilting books were written about the construction of quilts using many template cut pieces. With the "gift" of a rotary cutter and other cutting tools, we can make that same quilt in a fraction of the time. With busy lives and hectic homes, many women today prefer quilting techniques that bring a finished project in less time.

The strip pieced quilts that follow are perfectly suited to a beginning quilter. The construction techniques are basic. Once the 1/4" seam allowance has been achieved with accuracy, a beginner can tackle most all of the projects with confidence (I would reserve the Amish Pinwheel for a later project). Directions for a 1/4" seam test are included so that everyone has the advantage of accuracy.

The following quilts, arranged roughly in order of increasing "difficulty", are just the tip of the iceberg of quilts that can be made using these revolutionary strip piecing methods. Quilts selected for this book range from the readily recognized Snowball and Nine through more obscure patterns such as the Red Cross Postage Stamp and the Amish Pinwheel. There is sure to be a quilt for everyone.

Contents

About the Author

Brenda Henning is a compulsive quiltmaker with a fondness for traditional design and a desire to incorporate today's speed-piecing techniques with yesterday's well-loved patterns. Brenda's machine sewing experience began at the early age of 10 on her grandmother's treadle sewing machine with the first quilt following at age 14. Brenda became a compulsive quilter in the mid-80s, and began teaching quiltmaking in 1989, after her third child turned one.

Writing and self-publishing that work have been byproducts of teaching quilting. Brenda is the author of: *Alaskan Silhouette Sampler, Sampler Schoolhouse, Scrap Quilts for Material Girls,* *Stained Glass Flower Garden, Among Friends ~ More Scrap Quilts, Christmas Traditions in Stained Glass,* and *Birds of a Feather*, along with numerous individual patterns available under the label *Bear Paw Productions.*

Brenda lives in Anchorage, Alaska, with her husband, Richard, and their three children, Beth, Christi and Joshua. Two Rottweilers, Coco and Blue, (I'll bet you can't guess Brenda's favorite color!) share copious quantities of black dog hair with every quilt that leaves the premises.

Brenda teaches regularly at The Quilt Tree in Anchorage as well as for other shops and guilds throughout Alaska and the United States.

General Directions

Basic Supplies

Sewing Machine - in good working order, recently cleaned and oiled according to the directions given in your owner's manual. I find the problems new quilters experience are often due to the condition of their sewing machines rather than their quilting aptitude.

Sewing Machine Needles - I use size 70/10 for all piecing. This needle size leaves a smaller hole if "reverse stitching" is necessary. Start every project with a new needle.

Thread - Cotton thread is the best choice when sewing cotton fabrics. I use 50 wt./3 ply cotton thread.

Pins - Always a nice idea to have on hand. Personally, I use pins as little as possible.

Scissors - Three types of scissors are in my sewing room: heavy, sharp shears for cutting fabric; inexpensive paper scissors; and small, sharp tailor scissors for clipping threads at the sewing machine.

Seam Ripper - finely pointed and sharp.

Rotary Cutter - I prefer the Olfa® brand with new sharp blades. The larger 60 mm blade cutter is terrific for multiple layers.

Cutting Mat - Self-healing mat, at least 20" x 24", 24" x 36" if at all possible. I use Olfa® brand mats.

Rulers - an assortment of ruler sizes are used at my cutting table. When possible, I use Omnigrid® rulers because of their accuracy. 4" x 14", 3" x 18", 6" x 12", and 6" x 24" are the most commonly used sizes when I strip piece.

Fabric Basics

Selection

This can be the most fun part of the quilting process! While some of the quilts found in this book use just two fabrics, I find that I prefer the "scrap" look possible when making strip-pieced quilts. Why use 5 fabrics when 50 will work!?!

When making any of the quilts in this book, you may choose to use multiple fabrics to replace the single fabric called for. In the case of the "assorted" fabric strips, I generally will cut each strip from a different fabric. If that is not a possibility, divide the number of strips required by the number of fabrics available.

When selecting fabrics for a scrap look, choose fabrics that are of the same value, color or theme. Value can be defined as the lightness or darkness of a color. For example: in the **Red Cross Postage Stamp** the indigo blue fabrics are all very similar in color and value (darkness) of that color. **Nordic Star** uses four different values of the same blue. A range of fabrics could be used within the different values of blue that are required - multiple dark, medium and light blues rather than a single dark, medium and light blue.

The '30s reproductions are different colors, but they are reproductions from the same era. They stand as one in spite of their differences. The prints vary, the colors vary, but the theme is unmistakable.

Garden Tapestry and **Amish Pinwheel** are constructed using a single background fabric and assorted tone on tone prints. The values differ from one to the next, but the colored fabrics are from a collection of fabric - they are designed and colored to work together. As a result, the colors complement one another, creating a peaceful union of color. If the collection is large enough, you may be able to achieve a "scrap" look without departing from the collection. This is a great way to develop a scrap look without the mental anguish some quilters feel when selecting numerous fabrics.

Fabric Preparation

Fabric preparation should be handled in the same manner that the completed quilt will be cared for. I recommend prewashing all fabrics. As each piece enters my house, the first stop is the laundry room. All fabric in my personal stash has been washed using Orvus paste (a horse shampoo) or Dreft. Do not use detergent to wash your fabrics because detergents act to strip color from cotton fabrics.

To replace the firmness of the sizing that has been washed out of the fabric, **press all fabrics using a heavy spray starch or spray sizing**. The fabric that is prepared in this way will behave much better when pressing seams. Bias edges will be more stable and less likely to stretch. You will find that piecing is much easier with fabric that doesn't stretch out of shape so quickly.

Yardage

Yardage has been based upon 42" wide fabric. If your fabric is substantially wider or narrower after prewashing, your yardage requirement may need adjustment.

The cutting instructions given assume that the strips are cut from 42" wide yardage. **Fat quarters** may be used. Fat quarters are only 21" wide at best. At least twice as many strips need to be cut. A single subcut unit may be lost from each sewn strip set due to the fabric width of the fat quarters.

The yardages listed for each quilt pattern have been rounded up slightly. This will allow for the yardage end to be straightened after washing and for any accidental cuts that might be made.

Rotary Cutting Tools

The rotary cutter is a razor knife that resembles a pizza cutter. The blade is very sharp and deserves to be treated with utmost respect. This amazing tool has revolutionized quilt making, nearly replacing scissors. I recommend a rotary cutter that has a manual safety guard. Some rotary cutters available on the market have a spring-loaded guard that can accidentally retract when dropped, exposing the razor sharp blade and cutting your hand or foot. The spring-loaded guards protect you from only the most minor of blade "bumps." The rotary cutters that have a manually closing safety guard, such as Olfa® and Fiskar®, require that you consciously close the guard after every cut. Learn to make a habit of closing the guard every time!! An exposed blade on the work surface can lead to tragic results — accidentally cut fabric, or worse, cut fingers and bloodstained fabric. Do not leave a rotary cutter unattended around a curious toddler or young child.

I prefer to use the Olfa® rotary cutter. This particular rotary cutter can be used both right and left-handed without repositioning the blade.

The large blade rotary cutter is excellent for cutting many layers of fabric at once. The large blade measures 60 mm or approximately 2 3/8" in diameter.

To ensure the life of the blade, the rotary cutter must be used only on a compatible cutting surface. The self-healing cutting mats are a necessary tool. While the mats come in many sizes, purchase the largest cutting mat that you can afford. The 24" x 36" cutting mat is worth every dime. My cutting mat of choice is the Olfa® mat.

Omnigrid® is my ruler of preference. The Omnigrid brand is the most accurate of all rulers that I have worked with. It is very important that all of your rulers are accurate and agree with each other. Compare the markings of all rulers in your collection. If any ruler does not measure up, discard it!! **The markings on your rotary mat must also agree with the rulers you have chosen to use.**

Squaring Up Yardage

•Fold your fabric in half lengthwise, wrong sides together, selvage edges even. You may need to shift one selvage to the right or left to eliminate wrinkles along the folded edge. Once this has been accomplished, fold the fabric again, lengthwise, bringing the folded edge even with the selvage edges. The fabric will now be folded into four thicknesses, and measure about 10 1/2" wide, allowing strips to be cut without repositioning your ruler hand.

•Lay the folded fabric horizontally on your gridded cutting mat. The folded edge should be nearest you. Place the fold along a horizontal line of the mat. This will allow you to place your ruler along a vertical mat marking, guaranteeing a straight cut. If you are right-handed, the bulk of your fabric should be on the right, and you will start cutting from the left side. (Reverse for a left-handed person.)

•The rotary cutter is held with the blade perpendicular to the mat and against the edge of the ruler. The rotary cutter is held in the palm of your hand with the index finger on the ridged surface of the handle. This placement helps you to better control the rotary cutter. You are in effect pointing it in the proper direction.

•Cut away from yourself using one smooth even stroke. Do not make short choppy cuts which will create a ragged edge. The first cut will trim off the raw edge and square up the fabric. The clean edge will be perpendicular to the selvage. Trim sparingly to give the fabric a clean edge while wasting as little fabric as possible.

Cutting Single Strips

After the original cut has been made to square up the end of the yardage, you are ready to cut your first strip.

•Move the ruler to the right (left for a left-handed person) and align the squared off edge with the ruler marking for the strip width desired. Make sure that the correct marking lines up all along the cut edge, not just at one point!! Measure twice and cut once!!

•Cut along the right (left) side of the ruler. Be sure to keep your blade flush against the ruler; do not allow the ruler to shift. It may be helpful to hold the ruler with a finger or two off the left edge (right edge for a left-handed person). This will stabilize the ruler to prevent ruler slips. Lift the ruler and remove the strip without disturbing the yardage.

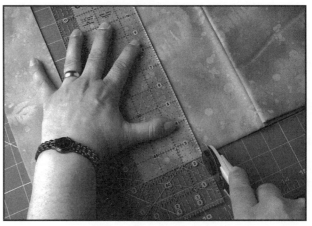

•Open the strip and look at it closely. The strip should be straight and of a consistent width. If your strip is not straight, refold your fabric and make certain that the edges are even. Also, make sure the original cut was made correctly, perpendicular to the folded edge.

The Dreaded Crooked Strip

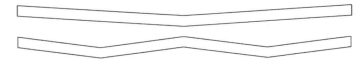

•If it is necessary to cut a strip wider than your ruler, use the rulings of the cutting mat to measure the strip or square. Double check the mat measurements against those of your ruler to determine if the mat measurements are accurate.

Cutting Multiple Strips

When it is necessary to cut many of the same size strips from a fabric, I use the rulings of the cutting mat. I must first double check the mat rulings against that of my rulers. Once it has been determined that all rulings agree, it is acceptable to use the rulings of my cutting mat.

•Fold the fabric as directed on page 6 under "Squaring Up Yardage".

•Lay the folded fabric horizontally on your gridded cutting mat. The folded edge should be nearest you. **Place the fold along a horizontal line of the mat.** (This will allow you to place your ruler along a vertical mat marking, guaranteeing a straight cut.) The raw edge should extend just past the "0" mark at the left edge of the cutting mat. If you are right-handed, the bulk of your fabric should be on the right, and you will start cutting from the right side. (Reverse for a left-handed person.)

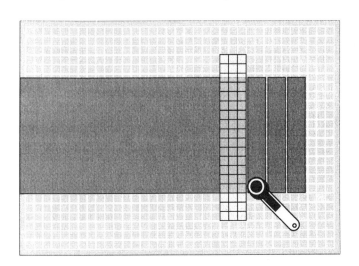

•The fabric strips will be cut according to the rulings of the mat. If your mat is 35" long, make a "cheat sheet" of the multiples of your strip width up to 35" - i.e. - 2", 4", 6", 8", 10" ... 30", 32", 34". These will be the cutting mat measurements that you will cut along. The "cheat sheet" allows you to cut without participating in mental gymnastics.

•You can find "cheat sheets" on page 72. This page can be cut from the book, or photocopied for your use.

Benefits of Cutting with Mat Rulings

•A larger segment of the fabric is "squared up". If you square the end of your fabric by placing the horizontal line of a 6" wide ruler along the fold, your fabric is square for only a 6" length. After cutting 6" worth of strips from the end of your fabric, you must square the end of your fabric once more. When the cutting mat is used, 24" to 36" of the fabric is placed along the horizontal ruling. You can safely cut this length of fabric before you must move the yardage and square the end once again.

•When cutting with a rotary cutter and ruler, it is not uncommon for the ruler to slip ever so slightly. If you are using the markings on your ruler to measure, and do not notice that your ruler has slipped, your minor slip may go unnoticed until much later. In fact, your ruler may slip slightly a number of times before you "square up" the end of your yardage again. This allows the minor slips to multiply and your cut strips to become the "dreaded crooked strips".

•If you had been cutting using the rulings of your rotary mat, that original slight slip would have been corrected with the next cut. Both resulting strips are still usable if the slip is truly minor. The subsequent strips will be straight.

•The cutting starts at the right end of your cutting mat (reverse for a left-handed person). The ruler is not lifted and the fabric strips not removed. The ruler is simply slid to the left and aligned for the next cut! Follow the cheat sheet for even greater ease.

•The greatest benefit is speed. This method allows me to cut many strips without having to stop and realign the fabric every 3 or 4 cuts. There is no need to square up the end every few cuts.

Subcutting Single Strips

•Squares and rectangles needed for piecing will be cut from strips. Cut the strip to the required width and open the double fold. You will be working with two layers of fabric and a single fold. If you are right handed, the selvages should be placed at the left. Trim off the first 1/2" to remove the selvages (more if needed) and square up the end of the strip. Use the mat markings to establish a perpendicular cut.

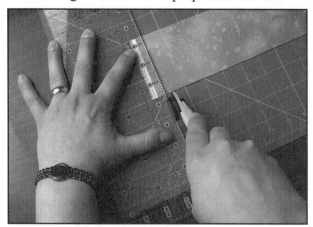

•Align the bottom edge of the fabric with a horizontal ruler marking. Place the desired ruler marking along the cut left edge of the strip. Cut the squares or rectangles to the required dimension. Continue cutting from the strip to satisfy the number needed.

Half Square Triangles

Half square triangles are literally triangles that are one half of a square. The square is cut once from corner to corner, diagonally. This places the grain of the fabric along the two short sides of the right triangle. Half square triangles are used whenever the short side of the triangle will fall at the edge of a quilt block or quilt top. This allows for the greatest stability and the least amount of stretch in these much handled positions.

Cut Once Diagonally

Fabric pieces that will be used as individual half square triangles will be cut as squares with the instructions to cut each square once diagonally as diagramed below. Cutting a square once diagonally places the stretchy bias edge along the long side of the triangle.

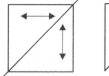

Quarter Square Triangles

Quarter square triangles are one quarter of a square. The square is cut twice from corner to corner, diagonally. This places the grain of the fabric along the long side of the right triangle.

Cut Twice Diagonally

Fabric pieces that will be used as individual quarter square triangles will be cut as squares with the instructions to cut each square twice diagonally as diagramed below. Cutting a square twice diagonally places the stretchy bias edge along the two short sides of the triangle.

1/4" Seam Allowance

All of our seams will be sewn with a 1/4" seam allowance. It is of utmost importance to establish and maintain an accurate 1/4" seam allowance. You will find a simple "1/4" seam test" at the right. The cutting instructions given for each piece refer to the actual cut size - the 1/4" seam allowance has been added to all dimensions. In the case of a quilt with a pieced border, the piecing of the body of the quilt will determine if the border fits properly! The measurements given are all mathematically correct; it is assumed that your piecing will also be correct.

I do not trust the 1/4" marking on my sewing machines. Usually the factory markings are accurate enough for clothing construction, but not for the precision demanded by quilting. I also do not recommend using the edge of your presser foot as a guide. Very few actually measure 1/4" from the needle.

You will actually be sewing with a **scant** 1/4" seam allowance. The difference will be taken up in the slight fold or "ridge" at the seam.

•To find your 1/4" seam allowance place a small ruler underneath your presser foot. When the needle is gently lowered, it should rest just to the right of the 1/4" mark on the right side of your ruler. If the needle were to pierce the ruler, the hole left by the needle would just graze the 1/4" ruler marking.

•With the presser foot holding the ruler in this position, carefully adjust the ruler so the markings on the left side of the ruler run parallel with the markings on the throat plate of your sewing machine.

•Once you are satisfied the ruler is positioned correctly, place a 1/2" x 3" strip of moleskin along the right edge of the ruler on the throat plate. Moleskin is a Dr. Scholl's® product, available at most groceries and pharmacies. The adhesive back of the moleskin will stick to the throat plate and give an edge to hold your seam allowance against. Moleskin gives more of an edge to follow than masking tape. It is not high enough that it will impede or pull out your pins.

1/4" Seam Test

•Cut 3 pieces of fabric 1 1/2" x 6". Sew these strips together along the lengthwise edge. Press the seams in one direction. After pressing, check that there are no "accordion" pleats at the seams. Press again if necessary.

•Measure your sewn unit; it should measure exactly 3 1/2" from raw edge to raw edge.

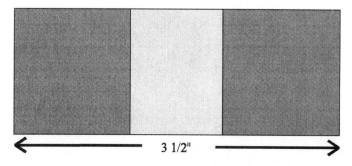

•If your sewn unit doesn't measure exactly 3 1/2" you will need to adjust your moleskin. If the sewn unit is **wider** than 3 1/2", your seam allowance is too narrow and the moleskin should be moved to the right. If the sewn strip is **narrower** than 3 1/2", your seam allowance is too wide and the moleskin should be moved to the left.

•The amount that you need to move the moleskin is only one fourth of the amount that your strip differs from 3 1/2". Two seams are involved in the sewn strip, each seam involves two pieces of fabric — move the moleskin 1/4 of the difference.

It is a commonly held thought that the 1/4" seam allowance should be measured to check the accuracy of the stitching. Unfortunately, this does not work. The seam allowance is a scant 1/4". Measure the **finished dimension** of the fabric from the right side of the unit or quilt block.

If you have placed the moleskin exactly as described, and are still having problems stitching a 1/4" seam allowance, it may be your sewing machine that is being naughty. The feed dogs of some machines pull to the right, some to the left. Sewing machines are an eccentric lot! Get to know your machine and work with its character flaws.

Strip Piecing

Not all piecing is accomplished by sewing individual squares and triangles together. The quilts in this book are all constructed by sewing strips together and subcutting the strip sets. The resulting units will be stitched together to form the intended square.

•The first step is to arrange the strips in the sequence they will appear.

•Begin by sewing strips together in pairs. This helps to reduce the arcing that can occur if strips are added to the strip set one at a time.

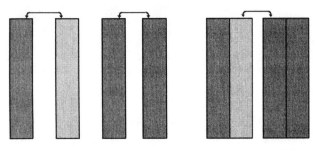

•After each pair is sewn, press the strips flat from the wrong side. This smoothes any wrinkles caused by poor thread tension. It also makes your strip moist (I always use steam when I am piecing) and pliable, so that the next pressing step goes more easily. You may have heard this called setting the seam.

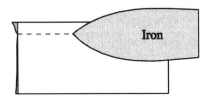

•Once you have set the seam, open the fabrics and press the seam from the right side. Pressing on the right side gives the visibility required to prevent accordion pleating at the seam. The seam allowances should be pressed in one direction for the greatest strength, generally toward the darker fabric. Watch for arrows to indicate the direction the seam allowance should be pressed.

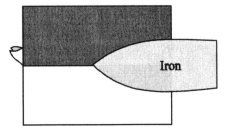

•Stitch strip pairs together and press.

•Press each seam as it is stitched rather than pressing all seams at one time to help prevent strip arcing.

Partial Strip Sets

All fabric strips cut will be cut from a 42" wide piece of fabric. Some of the quilt patterns that follow will ask for a partial strip set, i.e. 1/4 strip of a particular strip set. This means that you will need only 10 1/2" of a strip set, or perhaps less, to yield the required number of subcut units for that particular pattern. Strips have been cut to allow for that 1/4 or 1/2 strip set. If you choose to assemble a complete set, more strips will be needed to complete it.

Strip Set Subcutting

•Once sewn and pressed, the strips may be subcut into the units necessary to complete the piecing of the block.

•When subcutting the strip sets, the cutting mat is used to measure the strips.

•Place the strip right side up on the cutting mat. Align the lower edge of the sewn strip along a horizontal mat line. Use the vertical rulings of your cutting mat to subcut the strip into the units specified by your pattern. Use the appropriate "cheat sheet" listed on page 72 to speed the cutting. Be sure to place the strip end just past the "0" marking so that the selvages are trimmed from the end of the strip.

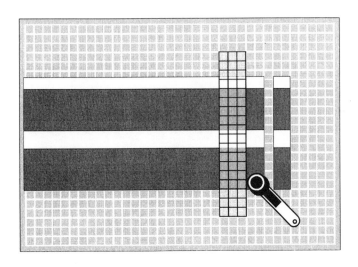

Layered Subcutting

To further speed the cutting process, multiple sewn strip sets may be layered.

•Place the first strip set along the 4" horizontal mat ruling. Carefully place the second strip set along the 3" ruling, a third set along the 2" ruling and a fourth set along the 1" horizontal ruling. Take care while layering the strips sets to not disturb the strips already on the mat.

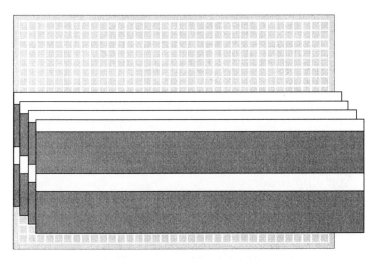

•Subcut the units using the vertical mat rulings. The cut made at the "0" ruler marking will remove the selvage. Use the appropriate cheat sheet from page 72.

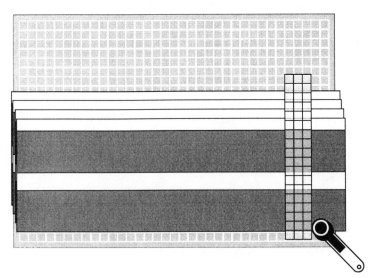

•Remember - when cutting layered sets, a cutting mistake has a much greater consequence.

Chain Piecing

•Chain piecing refers to the practice of stitching units one right after another without clipping the threads between the units. The first unit is stitched and left attached to the threads after passing under the presser foot. The second and following units are inserted under the presser foot one or two stitches after the previous unit has passed. No threads are cut.

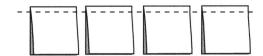

•This method saves thread and the time required to start each unit as an individual. It also allows you to repetitively piece the same unit and create a rhythm, thereby reducing mistakes.

•Clip the units apart and press.

•Reassemble the subcut units into the formation dictated by the pattern, stitch and press.

Borders

All of the quilts in this book were constructed using square borders. The application of a square border is easier to master than the application of a mitered border.

Primary Borders

Primary borders are all border strips that are attached to the quilt top before the final border. They may be very narrow or wide. All primary borders for the quilts in this text were cut as crossgrain strips and pieced together using diagonal seaming. Diagonal seams in the border strips are less visible than straight seams; no effort is made to place the seams in any particular position.

To make a diagonal seam, place the first strip right side up. Position the second fabric strip right side down on top of the first strip. The second strip will be placed at a right angle to the first. Stitch diagonally across the strip ends. Trim the excess to 1/4" and press the seam to one side. All of the "First (Second or Third) Border" strips are sewn together to create a long strip, and the necessary lengths are cut from it.

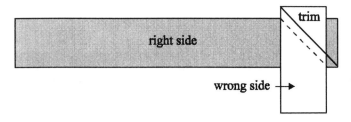

Pieced Borders

A pieced border is generally one of the primary borders. It is a wonderful addition to a beautiful quilt. A pieced border must be mathematically correct to fit the quilt top. If your piecing has been less that accurate, it is possible to adjust the vertical seams of the border strip to accommodate the difference. Unfortunately, this will also adjust where the points of the pieced border fall.

Final Border

The final border is cut from the lengthwise grain of the fabric. This will require extra yardage to be purchased, but it is well worth the expense.

The lengthwise grain of the fabric is more stable than the crossgrain. This extra stability will go a long way toward preventing stretching and ruffling of the quilt edge due to handling.

To cut a lengthwise fabric strip, measure the inches of fabric called for in the directions, and cut the yardage to that length. Fold the fabric crosswise, until it is narrow enough to be spanned by your rotary ruler. The folded fabric will have selvage at either edge. The first cut will be to remove the selvage. Cut the border strips to size. Use the rulings on the cutting mat if your ruler is too narrow.

Applying Borders

The individual quilt instructions in this book do not give exact measurements for the borders. **The strip measurements given are longer than what would be mathematically correct.** No matter how carefully you have pieced, over the course of many seams, variations do occur. It is not uncommon for the sides of a quilt top to have stretched with the handling that they have received, or even measure differently. These variations need to be addressed if you wish to have a square quilt that lays flat.

To accommodate the variations, do not cut a strip to the length that is mathematically correct, and do not stitch a long length to the side of the quilt top and cut off where the edge of the quilt lands!!!

Measuring

When adding borders it is important to measure the "body" of the quilt top, not the edges of the quilt where stretching may have occurred.

• Press the quilt top carefully. When measuring, it is important that the quilt lay as flat and smooth as possible.

• Measure from top to bottom through the

center of the quilt with a metal measuring tape. My sewing bag contains a petite 10 foot tape measure. Cut the two side borders to that measurement.

• Pin the border strips in place along the sides of the quilt top. Match the center of the border strip to the center of the quilt top. Use as many pins as necessary.

•Stitch the border strip to the quilt top. You are making the quilt top fit the border strip! Stitch with the border strip on top. The feed dogs will help to ease in the fullness of the quilt top if necessary.

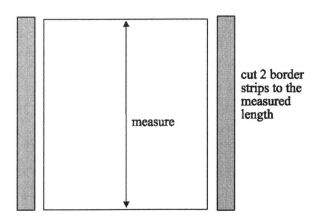

measure

cut 2 border strips to the measured length

• From the right side, press the seams toward the border strips.

•Lay the quilt on a flat surface and measure the quilt top from side to side through the center of the quilt, including the border pieces you just added. Cut the top and bottom border strips to that measurement.

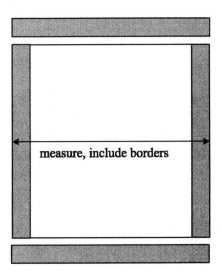

measure, include borders

•Pin and stitch these borders in the same manner the side borders were added.

•Press the seams toward the border strip.

All borders will be added in this manner. When applying the final border, backtack the seams that will be exposed at the raw edge of the quilt. This helps to prevent the stitches from pulling out as the quilt top is layered and quilted. The quilts in this book have had the side borders applied first, and then the top and bottom borders. This order of border application is generally a more economical use of fabric since a shorter yardage of fabric is required.

Batting

Batting is the layer of filling between the quilt top and the backing. There are many weights and types of batting available on the market today. It is available in polyester, cotton, cotton/polyester blends and even wool. Batting comes packaged in standard sizes or as yardage from a bolt. Some are better suited to hand quilting while others are best left for tying.

100% Cotton

Cotton batting gives a traditional look to your quilts. While traditional cotton batting needed to be quilted every 1/4" - 1/2" to prevent the fibers from clumping, today's cotton batting can be quilted up to 8" apart!

Cotton batting is my personal favorite. I prefer the antique look that the cotton batting gives. Cotton batting hand quilts nicely and is a great choice for machine quilting. As you select and purchase batting, my best advice is to read the package!! Know what you are working with to prevent disappointment.

Backing

How to prepare the backing is a matter of personal taste. Many quilters use the leftover scraps of the quilt top to piece together a scrappy backing. If you are planning to hand quilt the layers, a pieced backing may not be the best idea. The many seams might be difficult to "needle". Fortunately, fabric manufacturers are thinking about backings, and have made available fabric that is 100" - 120" wide. This fabric is very easy to use; simply cut to size. There are no seams to make the quilting process difficult.

Select a backing fabric that is a good quality cotton. Do not purchase a poor quality piece of fabric because it is less expensive. The backing needs to wear as well as the quilt top. A bed sheet really is not an ideal quilt backing. The fabric of a bed sheet is very tightly woven, and may make hand quilting a chore, perhaps even a painful experience.

The effect of the backing fabric color needs to be considered. If a polyester batting is used, a dark backing fabric may show through, dulling the light or bright colors of the quilt top. If the backing is patterned, the quilt top may appear splotchy! Cotton batting is more opaque and will allow less shadowing.

Yardage Requirements

Backing should be 6" - 8" larger than the completed quilt top. Yardage is figured on 43" of usable fabric width after preshrinking and removing the selvages. Measure the quilt top to determine the length and width.

- widths up to 37"   length + 6"

- widths 38" to 80"   (length x 2) + 12"
    Remove the selvages and sew one lengthwise seam. Press to one side.

- widths greater than 80"   (width x 3) + 18"
    Remove the selvages and sew two crosswise seams. Press to one side

Press the seam open if you plan to hand quilt.

Quilting

Quilting is the process by which the three layers of the quilt (top, batting and backing) are held together. Quilting can be accomplished by hand or by machine. And, if you have no inclination to quilt, the three layers can be held together by tying. Entire books are available on the subject of quilting, both hand and machine. I will refer you to your local quilt shop. They can help you find the text that you need.

Binding

Binding is the process of finishing the edge of the quilt after it is quilted.

Preparation

•Baste the edge of the quilt top down. This can be done with a long, wide zig-zag stitch on the sewing machine. This basting will prevent excess shifting of the quilt top layer at the edge as the binding is applied.

•Trim the batting and backing 1/8" beyond the raw edge of the quilt top. This extra fabric and batting will fill out the binding and prevent empty spaces.

•Piece the cut binding strips together using a diagonal seam as shown on page 12. Trim the seams to 1/4" and press the seams open.

•Press the long binding strip in half lengthwise, right side out, to a width of 1 1/4".

Attach the Binding

•Position the binding strips so that its lengthwise raw edges are even with the raw edge of the quilt top. Start stitching 1/4" from the corner of the quilt top, backtack to secure the seam and stitch to the opposite end. Stop stitching 1/4" from the quilt corner and backtack.

•Remove the quilt from the sewing machine, and snip threads. Rotate the quilt to prepare to sew the next edge.

•Fold the binding strip up, away from the quilt, it will fold nicely at a 45° angle. Fold it again to bring the strip edge along the raw edge of the quilt top, leaving a 2" - 3" tail of binding extending beyond the corner.   Lower the needle into the binding at the point where the first seam stopped (1/4" from the corner of the quilt top), backtack and stitch to the opposite corner of the quilt top.

•Continue around the quilt in this manner until you reach the corner where you began stitching. Fold the first section binding strip out of the way as you stitch to the end of the final binding length. Stitch to 1/4" from the corner and backtack.

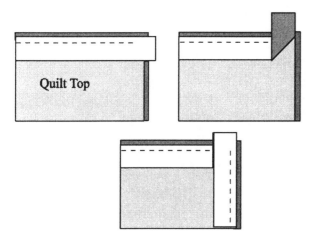

Mitered Corners

•To finish the corners of the binding, fold the tail of the binding so that it lays flat. Draw a line perpendicular to the seam line, starting at the end of the seam, **A**. Draw a second line at a 45° from the first line, **B**. Draw a third line, **C**, at a 45° from the opposite end of line **A**.   The intersection of lines **B** and **C** will be a 90° angle.

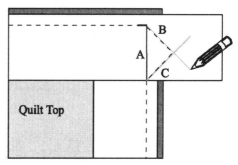

•With a small stitch, sew directly on lines **B** and **C**, pivot at the point, and backtack at each end of the seam. Trim to a 1/4" seam allowance. Turn the stitched corner right side out.

•Roll the binding over the raw edge of the quilt. Hand stitch the fold of the binding to the stitching line on the backside of the quilt.

Snowball and Nine

Lap Size Quilt Diagramed

Photo found on page 33.

Fabric Requirements

	Lap 65" x 76" 63 6" blocks	**Twin** 76"x 87" 99 6" blocks	**Queen** 87" x 100" 143 6" blocks
Background	5 1/2 yards	7 yards	8 1/2 yards
Purple	2 1/8 yards	3 yards	3 3/4 yards
Binding	3/4 yard	3/4 yard	1 yard
Backing	4 yards	5 1/4 yards	8 yards

Cutting Instructions

Background	Lap	Twin	Queen
2 1/2" strips	21 strips	31 strips	38 strips
2 1/2" squares	4 squares	4 squares	4 squares
6 1/2" squares	31 squares (6 strips)	49 squares (9 strips)	71 squares (12 strips)
2 1/2" x 6 1/2" rectangles	32 rect. (2 - 6 1/2" strips)	40 rect. (2 - 6 1/2" strips)	48 rect. (3 - 6 1/2" strips)
Purple			
2 1/2" strips	14 strips	21 strips	26 strips
2 1/2" squares	160 squares (10 strips)	240 squares (15 strips)	336 squares (21 strips)
First Border			
Sides	2 - 3" x 58 1/2"	2 - 2 5/8" x 70 1/2"	2 - 2 1/4" x 82 1/2"
Top and Bottom	2 - 2 5/8" x 51 1/2"	2 - 2 1/4" x 62 3/4"	2 - 2" x 74"
Final Border			
Sides	2 - 4 1/2" x 72"	2 - 4 1/2" x 84"	2 - 4 1/2" x 95"
Top and Bottom	2 - 4 1/2" x 69"	2 - 4 1/2" x 81"	2 - 4 1/2" x 92"
Binding			
2 1/2" strips	8 strips	9 strips	10 strips

Strip Piecing

1. Stitch 2 1/2"-wide background strip to 2 1/2"-wide color strips along the long edge. Press the seam toward the color strip.

Make:
Lap   11 1/2
Twin   17
Queen   21

2. To some of the strip sets from step #1, stitch a second 2 1/2" - wide strip of color fabric. Press the seam toward the color strip. This strip will be referred to as the positive strip set.

Make:
Lap   2
Twin   3 1/2
Queen   4 1/2

3. To the remaining strip sets from step #1, stitch a second 2 1/2" - wide strip of background fabric. Press the seam toward the color strip. This strip will be referred to as the negative strip set.

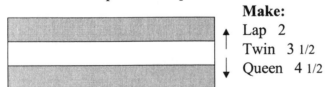

Make:
Lap   9 1/2
Twin   13 1/2
Queen   16 1/2

Set aside: Lap - 5 1/2, Twin - 6 1/2, and Queen - 7 1/2 **negative strip sets for pieced border construction.**

4. Place a positive and negative strip set right sides together. The seam allowances will be opposing.

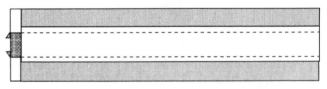

5. Trim the selvage from the strip ends. Cut the strip pairs into 2 1/2" segments. Each strip pair should yield 16 segments.

Cut: Lap   32 (2 strip sets)
Twin   50 (3 1/2 strip sets)
Queen   72 (4 1/2 strip sets)

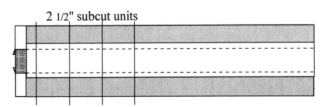

2 1/2" subcut units

6. Chain piece the subcut pairs. The pairs are cut with the seam allowances aligned and ready for stitching. Press the seam toward the positive unit.

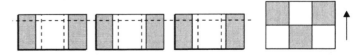

Make: Lap - 32, Twin - 50, Queen - 72

Nine Patch Construction

1. Trim the selvage from ends of negative strip sets. Cut the strip sets into 2 1/2" segments.

Cut: Lap   32 (2 strip sets)
Twin   50 (3 1/2 strip sets)
Queen   72 (4 1/2 strip sets)

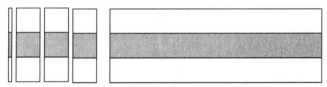

2. Assemble nine patch units using sewn pieces from step #6 on the previous page and the segments cut in step #1 above. Press the seam toward the positive strip.

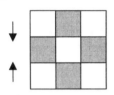

Make:
Lap   32
Twin   50
Queen   72

Snowball Block Construction

1. Sew and Flip Construction - Place a 2 1/2" square of colored fabric right side together on the corner of a 6 1/2" square of background fabric - raw edges even. Stitch from corner to corner of the 2 1/2" square as diagramed. Trim the seam allowance to 1/4". Press the seam toward the colored triangle.

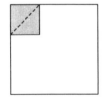
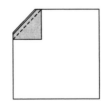

2. Repeat sew and flip construction on each corner of the 6 1/2" background squares.

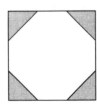

Make:
Lap   31
Twin   49
Queen   71

3. Partial snowball blocks - attach a 2 1/2" colored square to each end of a 2 1/2" x 6 1/2" background rectangle using the sew and flip technique. Trim the seam allowance to 1/4". Press the seam toward the colored triangle.

Make:
Lap   18
Twin   22
Queen   26

Pieced Border Construction

1. Trim the selvage from ends of the remaining negative strip sets. Cut the strip sets into 2 1/2" segments.

Cut: Lap   84 (5 1/2 strip sets)
Twin   100 (6 1/2 strip sets)
Queen   116 (7 1/2 strip sets)

2. Stitch together the pieced border units. Follow the diagram below. Remove a single background square from the end of one unit and move to the adjacent side of that same unit to complete the border strip. Press the seams in one direction.

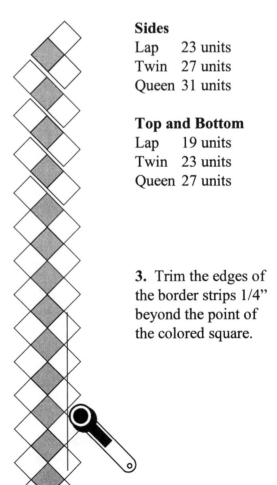

Sides
Lap   23 units
Twin   27 units
Queen 31 units

Top and Bottom
Lap   19 units
Twin   23 units
Queen 27 units

3. Trim the edges of the border strips 1/4" beyond the point of the colored square.

Quilt Top Assembly

1. Stitch the blocks together in rows, and sew the rows together to form the quilt top: lap - 7 x 9, twin - 9 x 11, and queen - 11 x 13. Watch the block placement closely to maintain the secondary pattern. Be sure to attach a partial economy block or a 2 1/2" x 6 1/2" rectangle of background fabric at each end of every row.

2. First border dimensions given are mathematically correct - this assumes that your piecing is accurate.

Attach side borders first and then the top and bottom borders. Press all seams toward the first border.

3. Stitch the pieced borders in place. Attach the side borders first and then the top and bottom borders. Miter the corner seam. Press all seams toward the first border.

4. Trim the final borders to fit and apply to the quilt top. Attach side borders first and then the top and bottom border strips. Press all seams toward the final border strips.

19

Stairway to Heaven

Lap Size Quilt
Diagramed

Photo found
on page 34.

Fabric Requirements

	Lap 69" x 87" 48 9" blocks	Double 87" x 96" 72 9" blocks	Queen 96" x 105" 90 9" blocks
Background	2 3/8 yards	3 3/8 yards	4 yards
Assorted Dark Blues	2 5/8 yards	3 3/4 yards	4 1/2 yards
First Border	5/8 yard	3/4 yard	3/4 yard
Final Border	2 3/8 yards	3 yards	3 1/4 yards
Binding	3/4 yard	1 yard	1 yard
Backing	5 1/4 yards	8 yards	8 3/4 yards

Cutting Instructions

	Lap	Double	Queen
Background			
2" strips - 4 patch	21 strips	31 strips	39 strips
3 1/2" squares	96 squares (8 strips)	144 squares (12 strips)	180 squares (15 strips)
Assorted Dark Blues			
2" strips - 4 patch	21 strips	31 strips	39 strips
3 1/2" squares	120 squares (10 strips)	180 squares (15 strips)	225 squares (19 strips)
First Border			
2" strips	7 strips	8 strips	9 strips
Final Border			
Sides	2 - 6 1/2" x 79"	2 - 6 1/2" x 88"	2 - 6 1/2" x 97"
Top and Bottom	2 - 6 1/2" x 73"	2 - 6 1/2" x 91"	2 - 6 1/2" x 100"
Binding			
2 1/2" strips	8 strips	10 strips	11 strips

Four Patch Units

1. Stitch each 2"-wide background strip to a 2-wide dark blue strip along the long edge. Press the seam toward the blue strip. Repeat with all 2"-wide blue strips.

2. Place two sets of sewn strips right sides together, reversing the colors as shown in the diagram. The seam allowances will be opposing.

3. Trim the selvage from the strip ends. Cut the strip pairs into 2" pairs.

2" subcut units

4. Chain piece the subcut pairs. The pairs are cut with the seam allowances aligned and ready for stitching. Press the seam to one side.

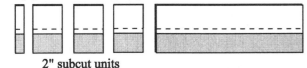

Make: Lap - 216, Double - 324, Queen - 405

Block A Construction

1. Using four patch units constructed at left, and blue 3 1/2" squares, arrange 9 patch units shown below. Pay close attention to the placement of the four patch units which will create the secondary design. Stitch the squares and four patch units together into rows. Press all seams toward the blue fabric as indicated by the arrows.

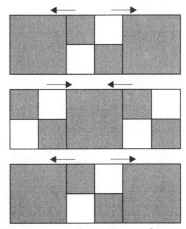

2. Stitch rows together. Press the seams toward the outer edges of the block.

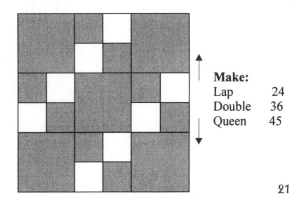

Make:
Lap   24
Double   36
Queen   45

21

Block B Construction

1. Using four patch units and 3 1/2" background squares, arrange 9 patch units shown below. Pay close attention to the placement of the four patch units. Stitch the squares and four patch units together into rows. Press all seams toward the background squares as indicated by the arrows.

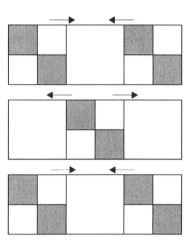

2. Stitch rows together. Press the seams toward the center of the block.

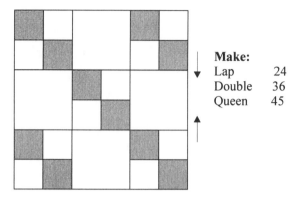

Make:
Lap	24
Double	36
Queen	45

Quilt Top Assembly

1. Stitch the quilt top together into rows, and sew the rows together to form the quilt top: lap - 6 x 8, double - 8 x 9, and queen - 9 x 10. Watch the block placement closely to maintain the secondary pattern.

2. Diagonally piece the first border, and cut lengths as needed. Attach side borders first and then the top and bottom borders. Press all seams toward the first border.

3. Trim the final borders to fit and apply to the quilt top. Attach side borders first and then the top and bottom border strips. Press all seams toward the final border strips.

Carrie Nation

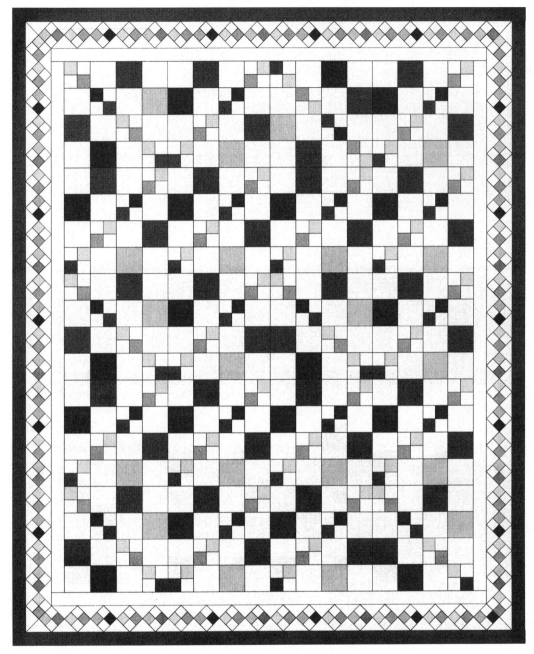

Double Size
Quilt
Diagramed

Photo found
on page 35.

Fabric Requirements

	Lap 64" x 80" 12 16" blocks	Double 80" x 96" 20 16" blocks	Queen 96" x 112" 30 16" blocks
Background	3 3/4 yards	5 1/8 yards	7 yards
Assorted Dark Fabrics	2 yards	2 3/4 yards	3 3/4 yards
Final Border	3/4 yard	1 yard	1 yard
Binding	3/4 yard	1 yard	1 yard
Backing	4 1/8 yards	5 3/4 yards	8 3/4 yards

Cutting Instructions

	Lap	Double	Queen
Background			
Small 4 patches			
2 1/2" strips	6 strips	10 strips	16 strips
4 1/2" squares	48 squares (6 strips)	80 squares (9 strips)	120 squares (14 strips)
Large 4 patches			
4 1/2" strips	6 strips	9 strips	14 strips
First border 2 1/2" strips	6 strips	8 strips	9 strips
Pieced border			
2" strips	7 strips	8 strips	10 strips
5 1/4" squares	32 squares (4 strips)	40 squares (5 strips)	48 squares (6 strips)
Assorted Dark Colors			
Small 4 patches			
2 1/2" strips	6 strips	10 strips	16 strips
Large 4 patches			
4 1/2" strips	6 strips	9 strips	14 strips
Pieced border			
2" strips	7 strips	8 strips	10 strips
Final Border			
2 1/2" strips	8 strips	9 strips	11 strips
Binding			
2 1/2" strips	8 strips	9 strips	11 strips

Block Construction

Small Four Patch Units

1. Stitch each 2 1/2" strip of background fabric to a 2 1/2" strip of dark colored fabric. Press the seam toward the dark strip. Repeat with all 2 1/2" strips specified for small four patch construction.

    Make: Lap   6
                        Double   10
                        Queen   16

2. Place two sets of sewn strips right sides together, reversing the colors as shown in the diagram. The seam allowances will be opposing.

3. Trim the selvage from the strip ends. Cut the strip pairs into 2 1/2" segments.

2 1/2" subcut units

4. Chain piece the subcut pairs. The pairs are cut with the seam allowances aligned and ready for stitching. Press the seam to one side.

    Make: Lap   48
                        Double   80
                        Queen   120

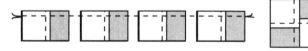

5. Stitch each small four patch to a 4 1/2" square of background fabric. Watch the placement of the four patch unit. If placed incorrectly, the secondary design will not develop. Press the seam toward the background square.

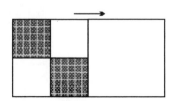

6. Stitch the units from step 5 together into larger four patch units. After the long seam is stitched, pull the two or three stitches of the vertical seam that extend past the long seam into the 1/4" seam allowance. This will allow the final seam to be swirled and pressed so that all of the seams are rotating in the same direction, distributing the bulk in the center of the block.

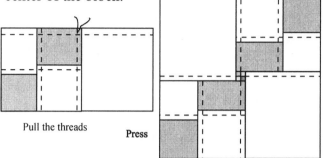

Pull the threads   Press

Large Four Patch Construction

1. Stitch each 4 1/2" strip of background fabric to a 4 1/2" strip of dark colored fabric. Press the seam toward the dark strip. Repeat with all 4 1/2" strips specified for large four patch construction.

Make:		
	Lap	6
	Double	9
	Queen	14

2. Cut strip pairs into 4 1/2" segments.

4 1/2" subcut units

3. Chain piece the subcut pairs. The pairs are cut with the seam allowances aligned and ready for stitching. **Swirl** the long seam as directed above.

Make:		
	Lap	24
	Double	40
	Queen	60

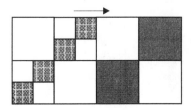

4. Join each small four patch unit (step 6 above) to a large four patch unit. Follow the diagram for placement. Press the seam toward the large four patch .

5. Join the units from step 4 to form the completed block. **Swirl** the long seam as directed in step 6 at left.

Make:		
	Lap	12
	Double	20
	Queen	30

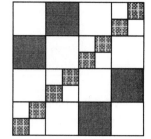

Pieced Border

1. Stitch each 2" strip of background fabric to a 2" strip of dark colored fabric. Press the seam toward the dark strip. Repeat with all 2" strips specified for pieced border construction.

Make:		
	Lap	7
	Double	8
	Queen	10

2. Cut strip pairs into 2" segments.

2" subcut units

3. Chain piece the subcut pairs. Press the seam to one side.

Make:		
	Lap	64
	Double	80
	Queen	96

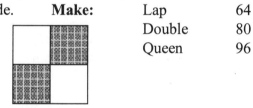

4. Trim each four patch unit from step 3 above using the trimming template below. Align the center lines with the seam lines when trimming.

Seam Line

Seam Line

5. Cut each 5 1/4" square of background fabric twice diagonally.

6. Attach a background triangle to one side of each **trimmed** four patch unit from step 4. Press the seam toward the triangle. **Set aside 4 units.**

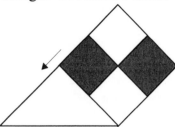

7. Stitch a second triangle to each four patch. Follow the diagram closely for proper placement. Press the seam toward the triangle.

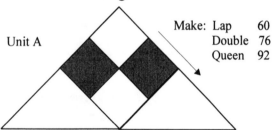

Unit A

Make: Lap 60
Double 76
Queen 92

8. To the 4 remaining units, attach a background triangle as diagramed below. Press the seam toward the triangle.

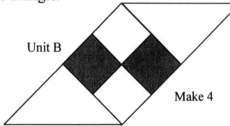

Unit B

Make 4

9. Stitch two pieced border units together to create the pieced corner unit. Press the seam to one side. Make 4 corner units.

Corner

Make 4

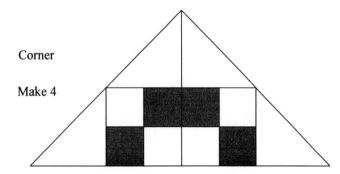

10. Stitch together the pieced border units. Follow the diagram below. Press the seams in one direction.

Sides		
Lap	15 A units & 1B unit
Double	19 A units & 1 B unit
Queen	23 A units & 1 B unit

Top and Bottom

Lap	11 A units & 1 B unit
Double	15 A units & 1 B unit
Queen	19 A units & 1 B unit

Lap Size
Borders
Diagramed

Quilt Top Assembly

1. Arrange the blocks on your floor or a design wall. This is the fun part. The blocks can be placed in any rotation and produce terrific secondary patterns. Stitch the quilt top together into rows, and sew the rows together to form the quilt top: lap - 3 x 4, double - 4 x 5 and queen - 5 x 6.

2. Diagonally piece the first border and cut lengths as needed. Attach side borders first and then the top and bottom borders. Press all seams toward the first border.

3. Stitch the pieced borders in place. Attach the side borders first, and then the top and bottom borders. Press all seams toward the first border.

4. Attach the pieced corner units. Press the seams toward the pieced corner units.

5. Diagonally piece the final border strips and cut to length as needed. Attach side borders first and then the top and bottom border strips. Press all seams toward the final border strips.

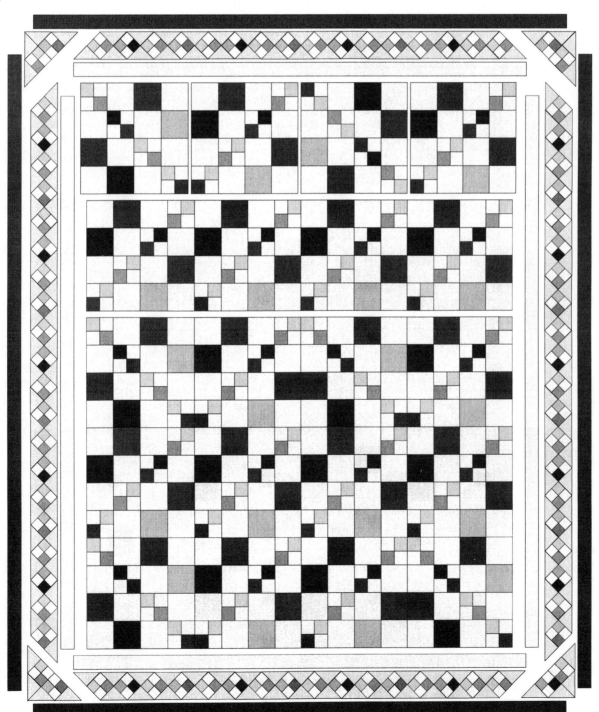

27

Garden Tapestry

Double Size
Quilt
Diagramed

Photo found
on page 36.

Fabric Requirements

	Lap 61 1/4" x 83 3/4" 15 11 1/4" blocks	**Double** 83 3/4" x 106 1/4" 35 11 1/4" blocks	**King** 106 1/4" x 106 1/4" 49 11 1/4" blocks
Background	3 1/4 yards	5 3/4 yards	7 3/8 yards
Colored Strips - assorted	1 3/4 yards	2 3/4 yards	3 3/4 yards
Border	2 1/2 yards	3 yards	3 1/4 yards
Binding	3/4 yard	1 yard	1 yard
Backing	5 yards	7 1/2 yards	9 1/2 yards

Cutting Instructions

Background

	Lap	Double	King
Background			
1 3/4" strips	26 strips	48 strips	63 strips
3" strips	1 strip	2 strips	3 strips
4 1/4" squares	26 (3 strips 4 1/4")	54 (6 strips 4 1/4")	72 (8 strips 4 1/4")
4 1/4" x 11 3/4" rectangles	24 (8 strips 4 1/4")	48 (16 strips 4 1/4")	64 (22 strips 4 1/4")
4 5/8" squares - corners	4 squares	4 squares	4 squares
Colors - Assorted			
1 3/4" strips	29 strips	53 strips	69 strips
Final Border - sides	2 - 6 1/2" x 76"	2 - 6 1/2" x 98"	2 - 6 1/2" x 98"
- top and bottom	2 - 6 1/2" x 65"	2 - 6 1/2" x 89"	2 - 6 1/2" x 110"
Binding - 2 1/2" strips	8 strips	10 strips	11 strips

Strip Piecing

1. Stitch 1 3/4"-wide background strip to 1 3/4"-wide color strips along the long edge. Press the seam toward the color strip.

Make:
Lap 18
Double 33
King 43

2. To some of the strip sets from step #1, stitch a second 1 3/4" - wide strip of color fabric. Press the seam toward the color strip. This strip will be referred to as the positive strip set.

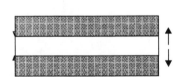

Make:
Lap 10
Double 18
King 23

3. To the remaining strip sets from step #1, stitch a second 1 3/4" - wide strip of background fabric. Press the seam toward the color strip. This strip will be referred to as the negative strip set.

Make:
Lap 8
Double 15
King 20

4. Place a positive and a negative strip right sides together. The seam allowances will be opposing.

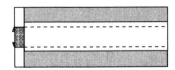

5. Trim the selvage from the strip ends. Cut the strip pairs into 1 3/4" segments. Each strip pair should yield 24 segments.

Cut: Lap 141 (6 strip sets)
Double 269 (11 1/4 strip sets)
King 353 (15 strip sets)

1 3/4" subcut units

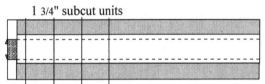

6. Chain piece the subcut pairs. The pairs are cut with the seam allowances aligned and ready for stitching. Press the seam toward the positive unit.

7. Stitch each 3" - wide strip of background fabric to a 1 3/4" - wide strip of color fabric. Press the seam toward the color fabric.

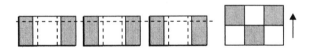

Make:
Lap 1
Double 2
King 3

8. Trim the selvage from the strip ends. Cut the strip pairs from step #7 into 1 3/4" segments. Each strip pair should yield 24 segments.

1 3/4" subcut units

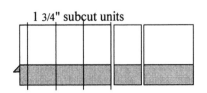

Cut:
Lap 24
Double 48
King 64

Nine Patch Construction

1. Trim the selvage from ends of the remaining positive strip sets. Cut the strip sets into 1 3/4" segments. **Cut:** Lap - 76, Double - 142 , King - 185

1 3/4" subcut units

2. Trim the selvage from ends of the remaining negative strip sets. Cut the strip sets into 1 3/4" segments. **Cut:** Lap - 41, Double - 79, King - 104

1 3/4" subcut units

3. Assemble positive and negative nine patch units using sewn pieces from step #6 on the previous page and the segments cut in step #1 and #2 above. Press the seam toward the positive strip.

Positive Nine Patch   **Negative Nine Patch**

Make: **Make:**
Lap 76   Lap 41
Double   142   Double 79
King 185   King 104

4. Assemble corner nine patch units using sewn pieces from step #6 on the previous page and the segments cut in step #8 on the previous page. Press the seam toward the unit just added.

Make:
Lap 24
Double   48
King 64

Block Construction

1. Triple nine patch block - assemble positive, negative and corner nine patch units together as diagramed below. Press the seams as indicated by the arrows.

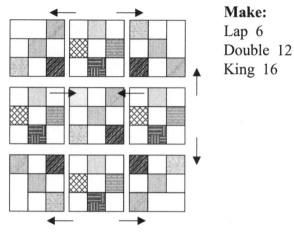

Make:
Lap 6
Double 12
King 16

2. Post block construction - assemble the positive nine patch units with 4 1/4" squares of background fabric as diagramed below. Press the seams as indicated by the arrows.

Post Block   **Partial Post Block**

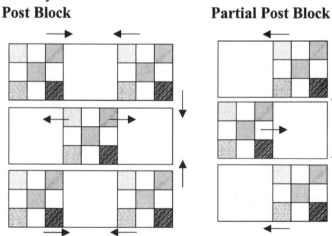

Make: **Make:**
Lap 2   Lap 6
Double 6   Double 10
King 9   King 12

3. Sash block construction - assemble positive and negative nine patch units together as diagramed below. Press the seams as indicated by the arrows. Attach 4 1/4" x 11 3/4" rectangles and press.

Sash Block   **Partial Sash Block**

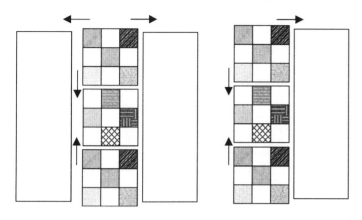

Make:
Lap 7
Double 17
King 24

Make:
Lap 10
Double 14
King 16

4. Corner block construction - cut each 4 5/8" square of background fabric once diagonally.

5. Cut additional 1 3/4" segments from the remaining strip pieces, and assemble the units below. Unstitch the segments to create the pieces necessary. Make 8. Press.

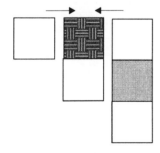

6. Trim the excess fabric that extends beyond the 1/4" seam allowance.

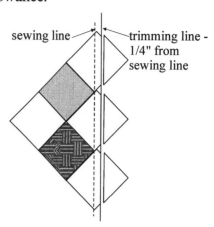

sewing line   trimming line - 1/4" from sewing line

7. Attach a 4 5/8" half square triangle of background fabric to each unit from step #5 above. Make 8.

Make 8

8. Assemble the corner square as diagramed below using the units from #7 above and the eight remaining positive nine patch units. Make 4 corner blocks.

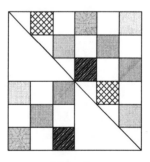

Make 4

Quilt Top Assembly

1. Stitch the quilt top together into rows and sew the rows together to form the quilt top:
lap - 5 x 7, double - 7 x 9 and king - 9 x 9. Watch the block placement closely to maintain the secondary pattern. Be sure to attach a partial sash or post block at each end of every row.

2. Trim the final borders to fit and apply to the quilt top. Attach side borders first and then the top and bottom border strips. Press all seams toward the final border strips.

Snowball and Nine, Brenda Henning, 1999; Anchorage, AK;
65" x 76". Pattern found on page 16.

Stairway to Heaven, Brenda Henning, 1999; Anchorage, AK; 69" x 87". Pattern found on page 20.

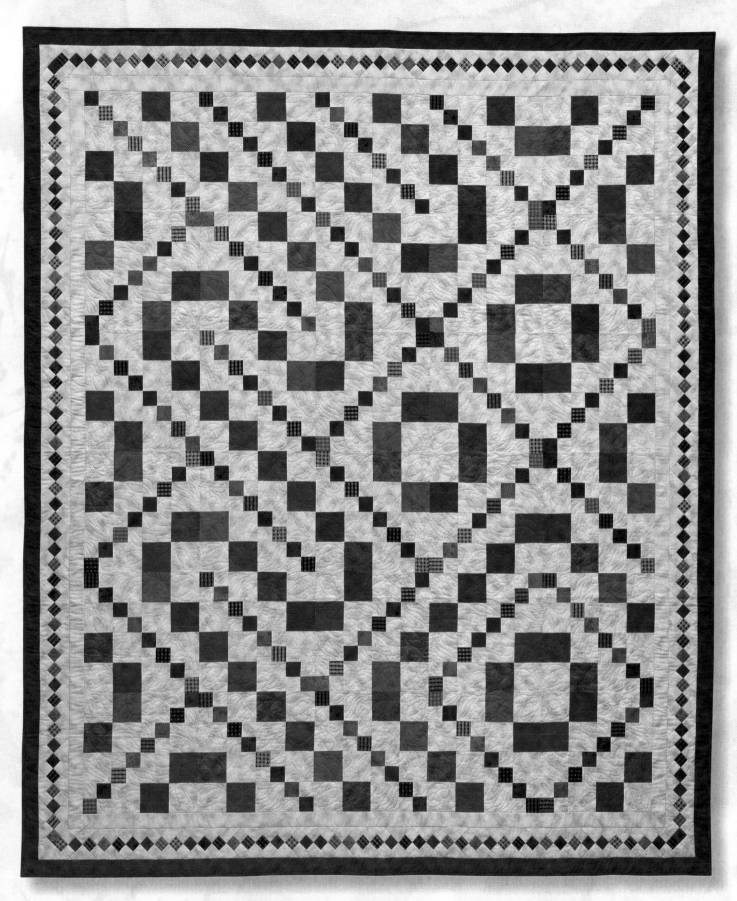

Carrie Nation, Brenda Henning, 1999; Anchorage, AK;
96" x 112". Pattern found on page 23.

Garden Tapestry, Brenda Henning, 1999; Anchorage, AK;
83 3/4" x 106 1/4". Pattern found on page 28.

Nordic Star, Brenda Henning, 1993; Anchorage, AK;
87" x 105". Pattern found on page 41.

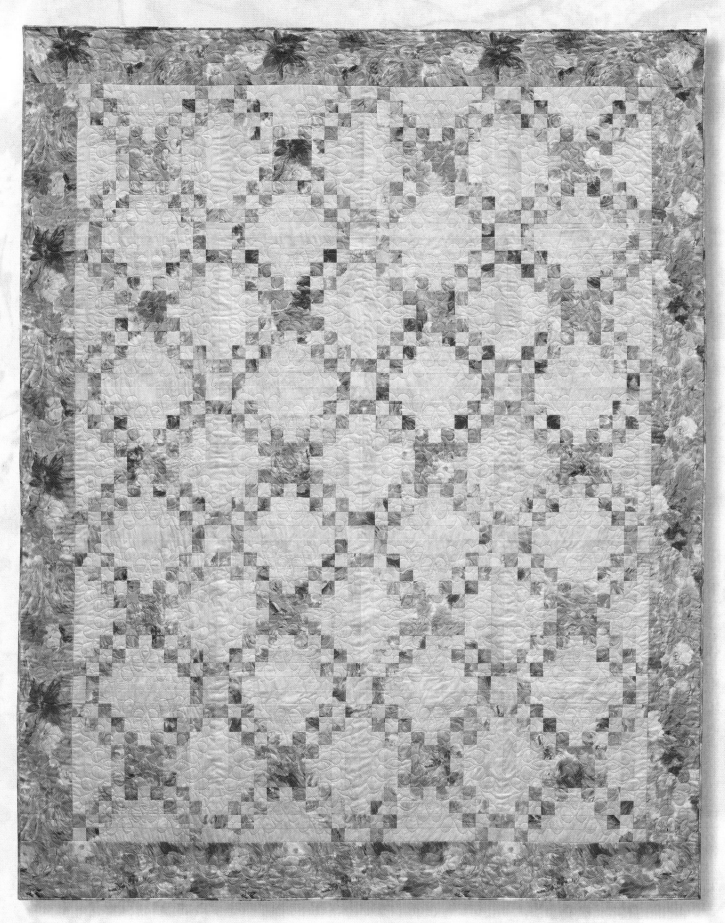

Whitehouse Steps, Brenda Henning, 1999; Anchorage, AK;
78" x 94 1/2". Pattern found on page 46.

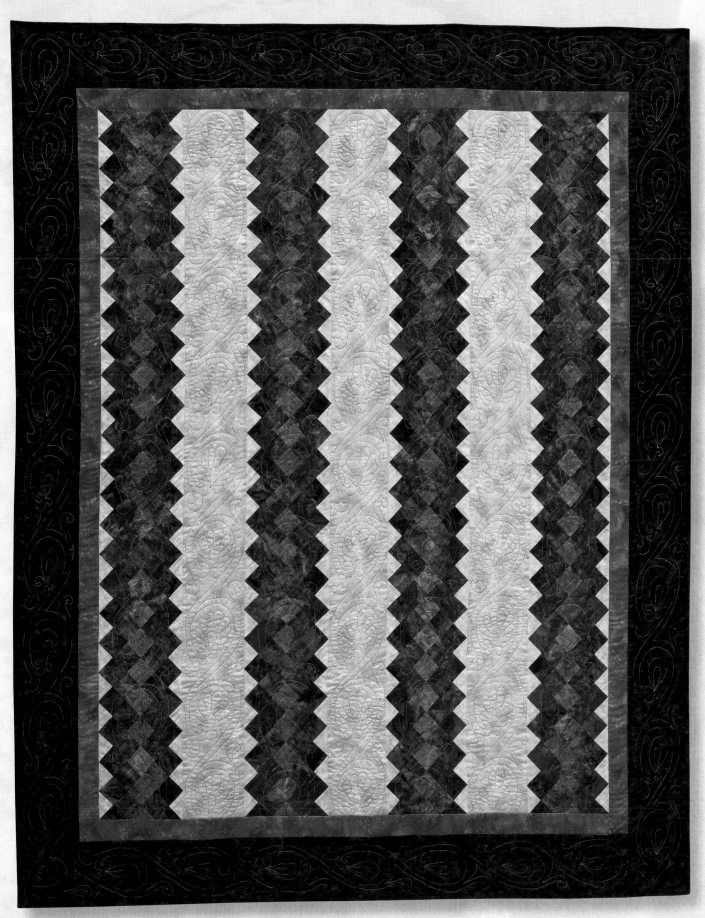

Cobblestone Path, Brenda Henning, 1999; Anchorage, AK;
68" x 84". Pattern found on page 51.

Stepping Stones, Brenda Henning, 1999; Anchorage, AK;
54" x 74". Pattern found on page 55.

Nordic Star

Queen Size
Quilt Diagramed

Photo found
on page 37.

Fabric Requirements

	Lap 51" x 69" 6 17" blocks	Queen 87" x 105" 20 17" blocks	King 105" x 105" 25 17" blocks
Background	2 yards	4 1/2 yards	6 yards
Dark, Medium Dark and Medium	1/2 yard each	1 1/4 yards each	1 1/2 yards each
Light	1/2 yard	1 yard	1 1/4 yards
Border	1 3/4 yards	2 3/4 yards	3 1/4 yards
Binding	1/2 yard	1 yard	1 yard
Backing	3 1/4 yards	8 yards	9 3/8 yards

Cutting Instructions

	Lap	Queen	King
Background			
1 1/2" squares	4 squares	6 squares	6 squares
1 1/2" strips	5 strips	13 strips	18 strips
3 1/2" strips	1 strip	3 strips	4 strips
5 1/2" strips	1 strip	3 strips	4 strips
7 1/2" strips	1 strip	3 strips	4 strips
11 1/2" squares	6 (2 strips)	20 (7 strips)	25 (9 strips)
Dark, Medium Dark and Medium			
5 1/2" strips	2 strips each color	6 strips each color	8 strips each color
Light			
5 1/2" strips	2 strips	4 strips	6 strips
Final Border - sides	2 - 7 1/2" x 52"	2 - 7 1/2" x 95"	2 - 7 1/2" x 95"
- top and bottom	2 - 7 1/2" x 48"	2 - 7 1/2" x 91"	2 - 7 1/2" x 110"
Binding - 2 1/2" strips	6 strips	10 strips	11 strips

Strip Assembly

1. Strip set 1 - Stitch 5 1/2" dark strips to each side of a 1 1/2" background strip. Press the seams toward the dark strips. Resulting strip should measure 11 1/2" wide. Subcut the strips into 1 1/2" units.

	Lap	Queen	King
Construct	1/2	1 1/2	2
Subcut Units	12	40	50

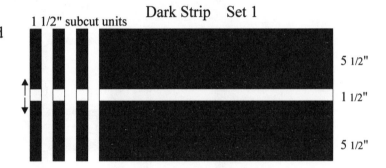

2. Strip set 2 - Stitch dark and background strips together as diagramed at the right. Press the seams toward the dark strips. Resulting strip should measure 13 1/2" wide. Subcut the strips into 1 1/2" units.

	Lap	Queen	King
Construct	1/2	1 1/2	2
Subcut Units	12	40	50

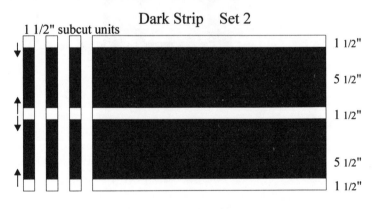

3. Strip set 3 - Stitch 5 1/2" medium dark strips to each side of a 3 1/2" background strip. Press the seams toward the medium dark strips. Resulting strip should measure 13 1/2" wide. Subcut the strips into 1 1/2" units.

	Lap	Queen	King
Construct	1/2	1 1/2	2
Subcut Units	12	40	50

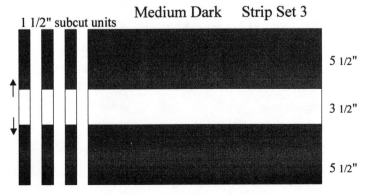

4. Strip set 4 - Stitch medium dark and background strips together as diagramed at right. Press the seams toward the medium dark strips. Resulting strip should measure 15 1/2" wide. Subcut the strips into 1 1/2" units.

	Lap	Queen	King
Construct	1/2	1 1/2	2
Subcut Units	12	40	50

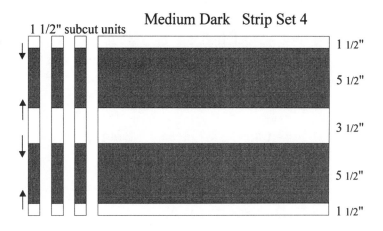

Medium Dark   Strip Set 4

1 1/2" subcut units

1 1/2"
5 1/2"
3 1/2"
5 1/2"
1 1/2"

5. Strip set 5 - Stitch 5 1/2" medium strips to each side of a 5 1/2" background strip. Press the seams toward the medium strips. Resulting strip should measure 15 1/2" wide. Subcut the strips into 1 1/2" units.

	Lap	Queen	King
Construct	1/2	1 1/2	2
Subcut Units	12	40	50

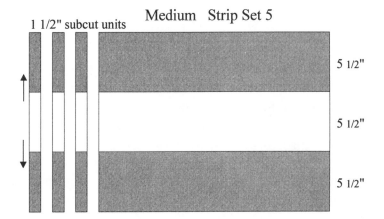

Medium   Strip Set 5

1 1/2" subcut units

5 1/2"
5 1/2"
5 1/2"

6. Strip set 6 - Stitch medium and background strips together as diagramed at right. Press the seams toward the medium strips. Resulting strip should measure 17 1/2" wide. Subcut the strips into 1 1/2" units.

	Lap	Queen	King
Construct	1/2	1 1/2	2
Subcut Units	12	40	50

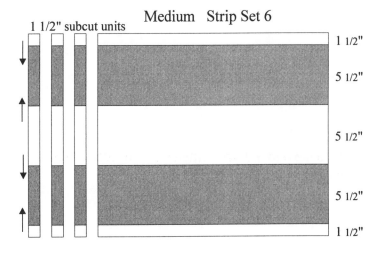

Medium   Strip Set 6

1 1/2" subcut units

1 1/2"
5 1/2"
5 1/2"
5 1/2"
1 1/2"

7. Strip set 7 - Stitch 5 1/2" light strips to each side of a 7 1/2" background strip. Press the seams toward the light strips. Resulting strip should measure 17 1/2" wide. Subcut the strips into 1 1/2" units.

	Lap	Queen	King
Construct	1/2	1	1 1/2
Subcut Units	9	25	30

Strip 7 will be used as sashing between the blocks.

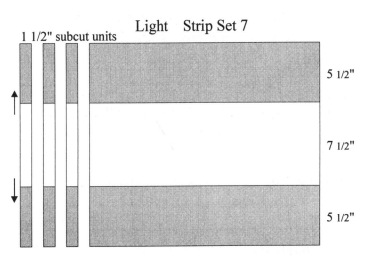

Light   Strip Set 7

1 1/2" subcut units

5 1/2"
7 1/2"
5 1/2"

8. Strip set 8 - Stitch light and background strips together as diagramed at right. Press the seams toward the light strips. Resulting strip should measure 18 1/2" wide. Subcut the strips into 1 1/2" units.

	Lap	Queen	King
Construct	1/2	1	1 1/2
Subcut Units	8	24	30

Strip 8 will also be used as sashing.

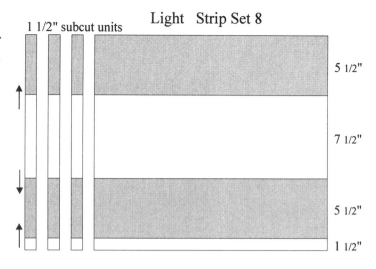

1 1/2" subcut units   Light   Strip Set 8

5 1/2"

7 1/2"

5 1/2"

1 1/2"

Block Construction

1. Stitch a **Strip 1** to two opposites sides of each 11 1/2" square of background fabric. Press the seams toward strip 1.

2. Attach **Strip 2** to the remaining two sides. Press the seams toward strip 2.

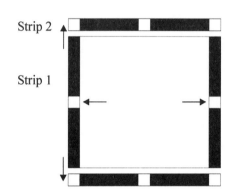

Strip 2

Strip 1

3. Stitch a **Strip 3** to two opposite sides of the square. Press the seams toward strip 3.

4. Attach **Strip 4** to the remaining two sides. Press the seams toward strip 4.

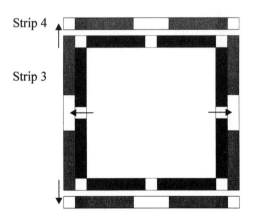

Strip 4

Strip 3

5. Stitch a **Strip 5** to two opposite sides of the square. Press the seams toward strip 5.

6. Attach **Strip 6** to the two remaining sides. Press the seams toward strip 6. The block will measure 17 1/2" when measured from raw edge to raw edge.

Make Blocks: Lap - 6, Queen - 20, King - 25

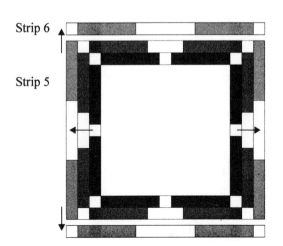

Strip 6

Strip 5

Quilt Top Assembly

1. Stitch the blocks together into rows, placing Strip 7 between blocks and at the row ends as diagramed. Stitch and press the seams toward Strip 7.
Lap - 2 x 3, Queen - 4 x 5, and King - 5 x 5.

2. Join Strip 8 units together into rows to form sashing. Add a single 1 1/2" background square to the end of each row. Press all seams toward the Strip 8.

3. Assemble rows of blocks with rows of sashing between them. Press the long seams toward the sashing strips.

4. Trim final borders to fit and apply to the quilt top. Attach side borders first and then the top and bottom borders. Press all seams toward the final border strips.

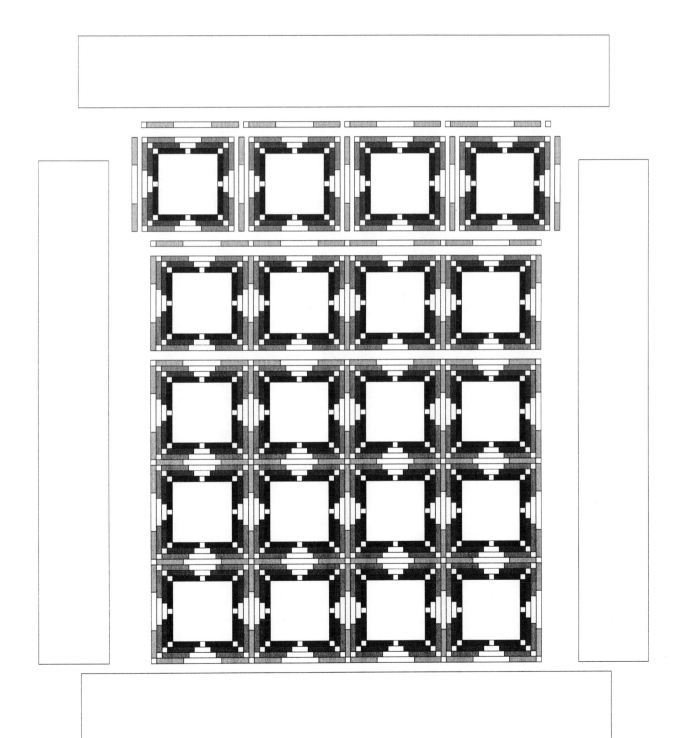

Whitehouse Steps

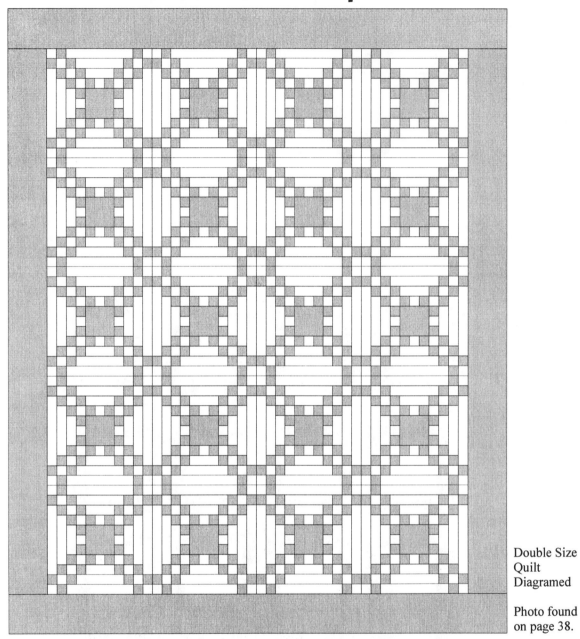

Double Size
Quilt
Diagramed

Photo found
on page 38.

Fabric Requirements

	Lap 61 1/2" x 78" 12 16 1/2" blocks	Double 78" x 94 1/2" 20 16 1/2" blocks	Queen 94 1/2" x 111" 30 16 1/2" blocks
Background	3 yards	4 1/4 yards	6 yards
Medium Print	1 5/8 yards	2 1/4 yards	3 5/8 yards
Border	2 1/4 yards	2 1/2 yards	3 yards
Binding	3/4 yard	3/4 yard	1 yard
Backing	4 1/8 yards	6 yards	8 3/4 yards

Cutting Instructions

	Lap	Double	Queen
Background			
2" strips	13 strips	20 strips	30 strips
5" strips	3 strips	4 strips	6 strips
8" strips	3 strips	4 strips	6 strips
11" strips	3 strips	4 strips	6 strips
Medium Print			
2" strips	20 strips	32 strips	48 strips
5" squares	12 (2 strips)	20 (3 strips)	30 (4 strips)
Final Border - sides	2 - 6 1/2" x 70"	2 - 6 1/2" x 86"	2 - 6 1/2" x 103"
- top and bottom	2 - 6 1/2" x 65"	2 - 6 1/2" x 82"	2 - 6 1/2" x 98"
Binding - 2 1/2" strips	7 strips	9 strips	11 strips

Strip Assembly

1. Strip set 1 - Stitch 2" medium strips to each side of a 2" background strip. Press the seams toward the medium strips. Resulting strip should measure 5" wide. Subcut the strips into 2" units.

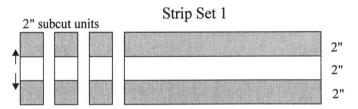

	Lap	Double	Queen
Construct	1 1/4	2	3
Subcut Units	24	40	60

2. Strip set 2 - Stitch medium and background strips together as diagramed at the right. Press the seams toward the medium strips. Resulting strip should measure 8" wide. Subcut the strips into 2" units.

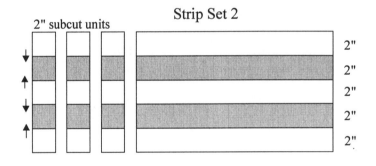

	Lap	Double	Queen
Construct	1 1/4	2	3
Subcut Units	24	40	60

3. Strip set 3 - Stitch 2" medium strips to each side of a 5" background strip. Press the seams toward the medium strips. Resulting strip should measure 8" wide. Subcut the strips into 2" units.

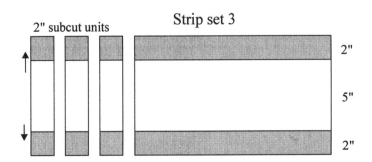

	Lap	Double	Queen
Construct	1 1/4	2	3
Subcut Units	24	40	60

4. Strip set 4 - Stitch medium and background strips together as diagramed at right with a 5" background strip at the center. Press the seams toward the medium strips. Resulting strip should measure 11" wide. Subcut the strips into 2" units.

	Lap	Double	Queen
Construct	1 1/4	2	3
Subcut Units	24	40	60

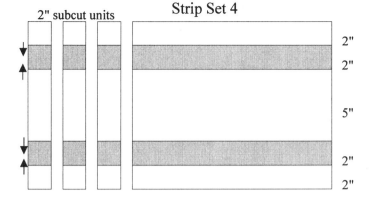

5. Strip set 5 - Stitch 2" medium strips to each side of a 8" background strip. Press the seams toward the medium strips. Resulting strip should measure 11" wide. Subcut the strips into 2" units.

	Lap	Double	Queen
Construct	1 1/4	2	3
Subcut Units	24	40	60

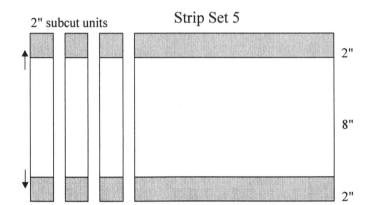

6. Strip set 6 - Stitch medium and background strips together as diagramed at right with an 8" background strip at the center. Press the seams toward the medium strips. Resulting strip should measure 14" wide. Subcut the strips into 2" units.

	Lap	Double	Queen
Construct	1 1/4	2	3
Subcut Units	24	40	60

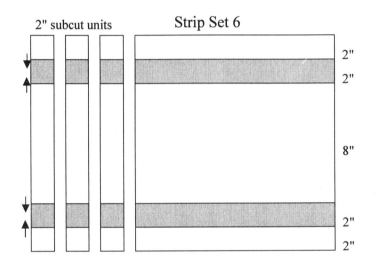

7. Strip set 7 - Stitch 2" medium strips to each side of an 11" background strip. Press the seams toward the medium strips. Resulting strip should measure 14" wide. Subcut the strips into 2" units.

	Lap	Double	Queen
Construct	1 1/4	2	3
Subcut Units	24	40	60

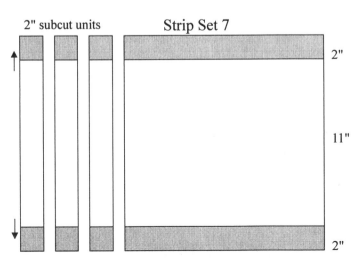

8. Strip set 8 - Stitch medium and background strips together as diagramed at right with an 11" background strip at the center. Press the seams toward the medium strips. Resulting strip should measure 17" wide. Subcut the strips into 2" units.

	Lap	Double	Queen
Construct	1 1/4	2	3
Subcut Units	24	40	60

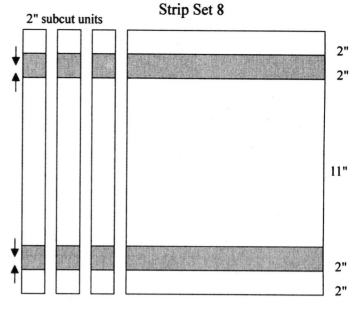

2" subcut units

Strip Set 8

2"
2"

11"

2"
2"

Block Construction

1. Stitch a **Strip 1** to two opposites sides of each 5" square of medium print fabric. Press the seams toward strip 1.

2. Attach **Strip 2** to the remaining two sides. Press the seams away from strip 2.

3. Continue adding strips in this manner until each block has received all eight strips. Press all seams according to the direction indicated by the arrows.

Make Blocks: Lap - 12, Double - 20, Queen - 30

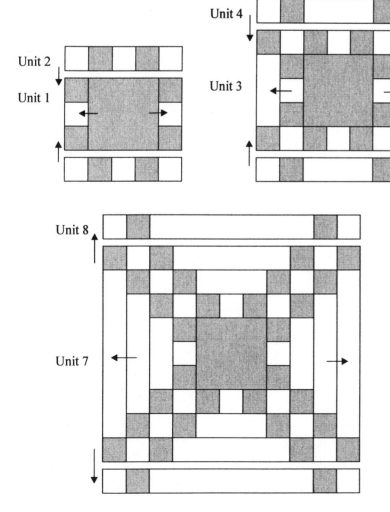

Unit 2

Unit 1

Unit 4

Unit 3

Unit 6

Unit 5

Unit 8

Unit 7

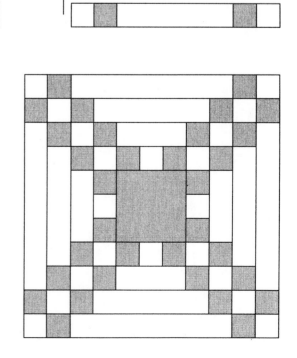

Quilt Top Assembly

1. Stitch the blocks together into rows. Sew the rows together to form the quilt top. Lap - 3 x 4, Double - 4 x 5, and Queen - 5 x 6.

2. Trim final borders to fit and apply to the quilt top. Attach side borders first and then the top and bottom borders. Press all seams toward the final border strips.

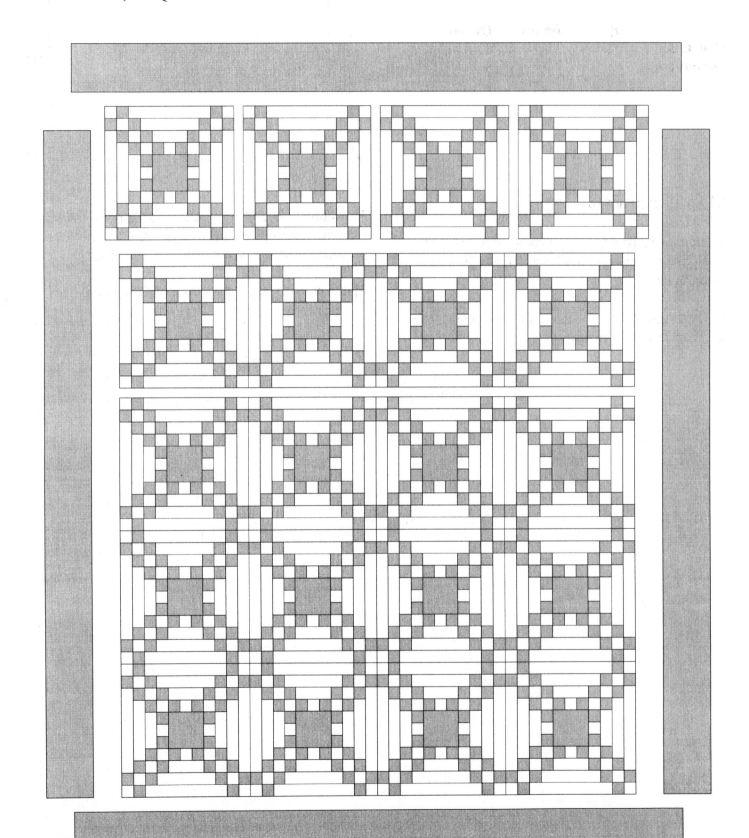

Cobblestone Path

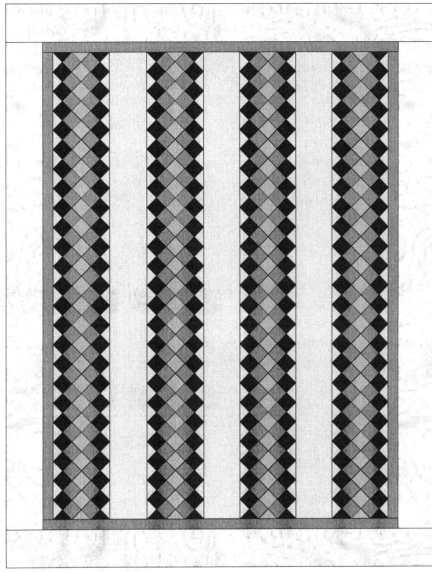

Lap Size Quilt
Diagramed

Photo found
on page 39.

Fabric Requirements

	Lap 68" x 84" 4 strips 24 units long	**Double** 82 1/2" x 92 1/2" 5 strips 27 units long	**Queen** 97" x 101" 6 strips 30 units long
Background	1 1/8 yards	1 1/2 yards	2 1/8 yards
Dark Blue	1 1/8 yards	1 1/2 yards	2 1/8 yards
Medium	1 1/8 yards	1 1/2 yards	2 1/8 yards
Light	3/4 yard	3/4 yard	1 yard
Plain Bar	2 1/4 yards	2 1/2 yards	2 3/4 yards
First Border	3/4 yard	3/4 yard	3/4 yard
Final Border	2 1/4 yards	2 3/4 yards	3 yards
Backing	5 1/8 yards	7 1/2 yards	8 3/4 yards
Binding	3/4 yard	3/4 yard	1 yard

Cutting Instructions

		Lap	**Double**	**Queen**
Background	2 1/2" strips	13 strips	18 strips	24 strips
Dark Blue	2 1/2" strips	13 strips	18 strips	24 strips
Medium	2 1/2" strips	13 strips	18 strips	24 strips
Light	2 1/2" strips	7 strips	9 strips	12 strips
Plain Bars				
6 1/2" strips - lengthwise cut		3 strips 72" long	4 strips 80" long	5 strips 89" long
First Border	2 1/2" strips	7 strips	8 strips	9 strips
Final Border - sides		2 - 6 1/2" x 76"	2 - 6 1/2" x 85"	2 - 6 1/2" x 93"
- top and bottom		2 - 6 1/2" x 72"	2 - 6 1/2" x 86"	2 - 6 1/2" x 101"
Binding - 2 1/2" strips		8 strips	9 strips	10 strips

Strip Assembly

1. Stitch 2 1/2" colored strips together in the order diagramed at right. Press the seams as indicated by the arrows. Resulting strip should measure 14 1/2" wide. Trim the selvages from the strip end. Subcut the sewn strips into 2 1/2" units.

2 1/2" subcut units

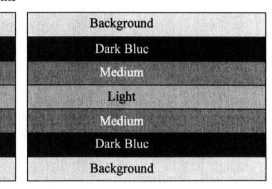

	Lap	**Double**	**Queen**
Construct	6 1/2	9	12
Subcut Units	100	140	186

2. Cobblestone Path Construction Reassemble the cut units as diagramed at right, offsetting the colors. Seam allowances will oppose. Gently press seams in one direction.

	Lap	**Double**	**Queen**
# of Paths	4	5	6
Subcut Units	23	26	29

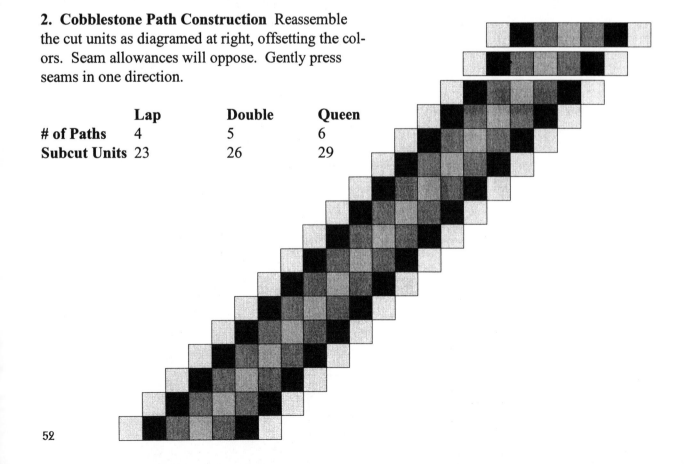

4. Corner Construction Cut individual units as diagramed below.

	Lap	**Double**	**Queen**
Cut Units	8	10	12

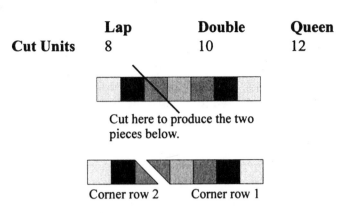

Cut here to produce the two pieces below.

Corner row 2   Corner row 1

5. Arrange the cut units as diagramed below and stitch together creating the corner units. Two corner units are made for each cobblestone path.

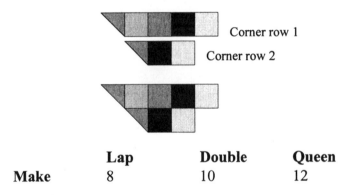

Corner row 1

Corner row 2

	Lap	**Double**	**Queen**
Make	8	10	12

6. Attach a corner unit to each end of the cobblestone paths. Press all long seams in one direction.

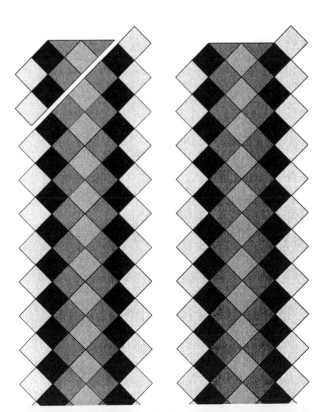

7. Trim the excess fabric that extends beyond the 1/4" seam allowance along the cobblestone path sides and path ends as diagramed below. The dotted line indicates the position of the seam.

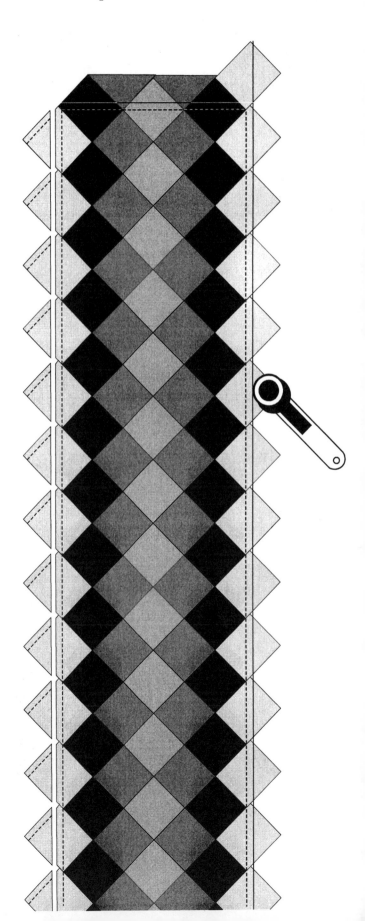

Quilt Top Assembly

1. Carefully measure the length of the cobblestone paths and trim the plain bars accordingly. All bars will be cut the same length. Handle the pieced strips with care to prevent stretching.

2. Stitch cobblestone paths and plain bars together alternately. Press the seams toward the plain bars.

3. Diagonally piece the first border and cut lengths as needed. Attach side borders first and then the top and bottom borders. Press all seams toward the first border.

4. Trim final borders to fit and apply to the quilt top. Attach side borders first and then the top and bottom borders. Press all seams toward the final border strips.

Stepping Stones

Lap Size Quilt
Diagramed

Photo found
on page 40.

Fabric Requirements

	Lap 54" x 74" 24 pieced units	Double 74" x 94" 48 pieced units	Queen 94" x 114" 80 pieced units
Light Cream	1 1/8 yards	2 1/4 yards	3 1/4 yards
Dark Blue	1 yard	1 1/2 yards	2 3/8 yards
Dark Gold	2 1/4 yards	3 1/2 yards	5 3/4 yards
First Border - Rust	1/2 yard	1/2 yard	2/3 yard
Final Border - Multi-Print	2 1/4 yards	2 3/4 yards	3 1/4 yards
Backing	3 1/2 yards	5 3/4 yards	8 1/2 yards
Binding	3/4 yard	3/4 yard	1 yard

Cutting Instructions

		Lap	Double	Queen
Light Cream	2 1/2" strips	6 strips	12 strips	20 strips
	3 1/2" strips	5 strips	9 strips	15 strips
Dark Blue	2 1/2" strips	9 strips	18 strips	30 strips
Dark Gold	2 1/2" strips	3 strips	6 strips	10 strips
	9" squares	8 squares (2 strips)	18 squares (5 strips)	32 squares (8 strips)
	6 1/8" squares	7 squares (2 strips)	17 squares (3 strips)	31 squares (7 strips)
A Triangle	13 1/4" squares	2 squares	3 squares	4 squares (2 strips)
	Cut the 13 1/4" squares twice diagonally			
B Triangle	9 1/4" squares	3 squares	4 squares	5 squares (2 strips)
	Cut the 9 1/4" squares twice diagonally			
C - Corner	7" squares	2 squares	2 squares	2 squares
	Cut the 7" squares once diagonally			
First Border -	1 1/2" strips	6 strips	8 strips	10 strips
Final Border - sides		2 - 6 1/2" x 67"	2 - 6 1/2" x 87"	2 - 6 1/2" x 107"
	- top and bottom	2 - 6 1/2" x 58"	2 - 6 1/2" x 78"	2 - 6 1/2" x 99"
Binding - 2 1/2" strips		7 strips	9 strips	11 strips

Strip Assembly

1. Strip set 1 - Stitch strips together in the order diagramed at right. Press the seams toward the dark blue strips. Resulting strip should measure 11 1/2" wide. Trim the selvage from the strip ends. Subcut the strips into 2 1/2" units.

	Lap	Double	Queen
Construct	3	6	10
Subcut Units	48	96	160

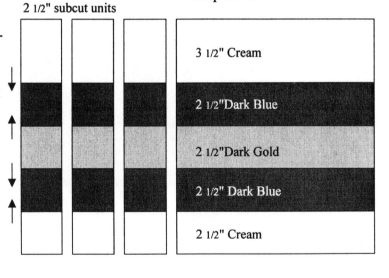

2 1/2" subcut units

Strip Set 1

- 3 1/2" Cream
- 2 1/2" Dark Blue
- 2 1/2" Dark Gold
- 2 1/2" Dark Blue
- 2 1/2" Cream

2. Strip set 2 - Stitch strips together in the order diagramed at right. Press the seams toward the dark blue strips. Resulting strip should measure 11 1/2" wide. Trim the selvage from the strip ends. Subcut the strips into 2 1/2" units.

	Lap	Double	Queen
Construct	1 1/2	3	5
Subcut Units	24	48	80

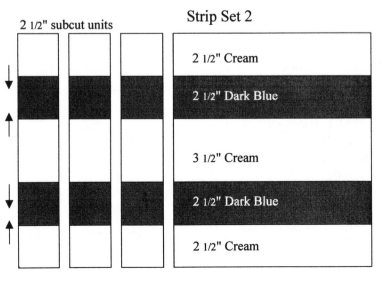

2 1/2" subcut units

Strip Set 2

- 2 1/2" Cream
- 2 1/2" Dark Blue
- 3 1/2" Cream
- 2 1/2" Dark Blue
- 2 1/2" Cream

3. Stepping Stone Construction - Reassemble the cut units as diagramed below, offsetting the colors. Rotate unit 1 as necessary to place the 3 1/2" segments adjacent to one another. Gently press seams in one direction. Add units to the strip until the strip is 6 - 8 feet long.

4. Make a trimming template from a sheet of transparent template plastic. Cut the template to measure 6 1/8" x 9". Mark the horizontal and vertical center with a line.

5. Place the template on the sewn strip as diagramed below. Trim away the excess from around the template creating your first stepping stone. **Reserve the "waste" triangle cut from the beginning of the strip. Set aside to be used later.** Continue cutting stepping stones from the strip until you approach the end of the strip.

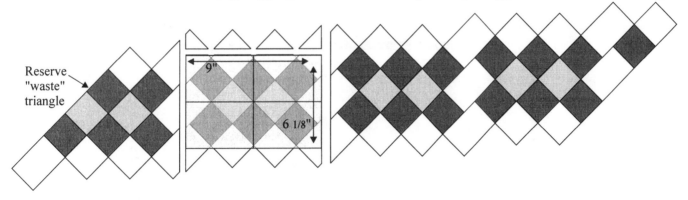

6. Stitch additional units 1 and 2 to the end of the strip until it is 6 - 8 feet long, press, and repeat the cutting process. Continue in this manner until you have used all of the cut units 1 and 2.

7. After cutting stepping stones from the sewn strip, stitch the "waste" segment to the end of the strip. This will create the last two stepping stones. Trim the stepping stones from this final strip segment.

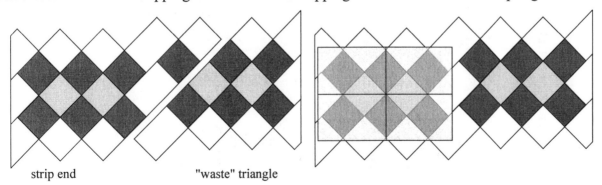

strip end   "waste" triangle

Make: Lap - 24, Double - 48, Queen - 80

Quilt Top Assembly - Lap Size

1. Lay the quilt top out on a floor or design wall. The triangles are easy to rotate into an incorrect position. The quilt top will be assembled in diagonal rows. Join pieces together into rows. Press all seams toward the unpieced squares and triangles.

2. Stitch rows together and press long seams in one direction.

3. Continue to assemble the quilt top in this manner. Attach the corner triangles last.

4. Diagonally piece the first border strips together, cut lengths as needed and apply to the quilt. Attach the side borders first and then the top and bottom borders. Press seams toward the border strips.

5. Trim final borders to fit and apply to the quilt top. Attach side borders first and then the top and bottom borders. Press all seams toward the final border.

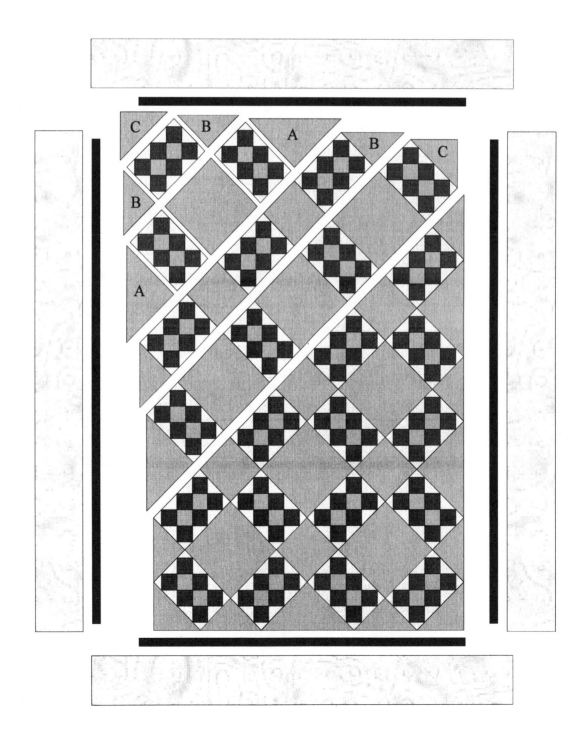

Quilt Top Assembly Diagram - Double

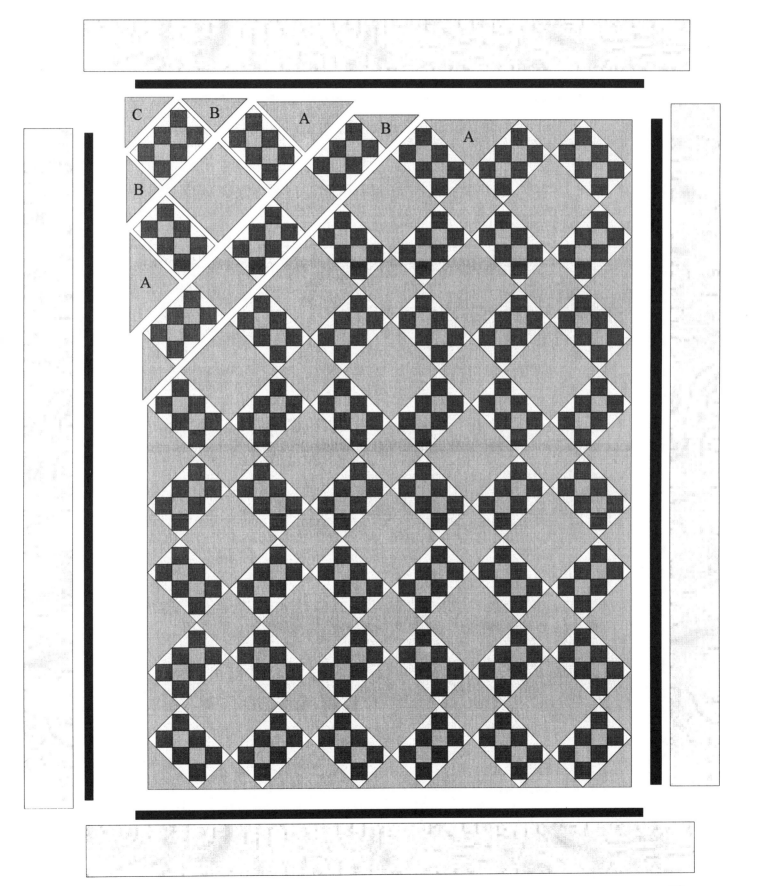

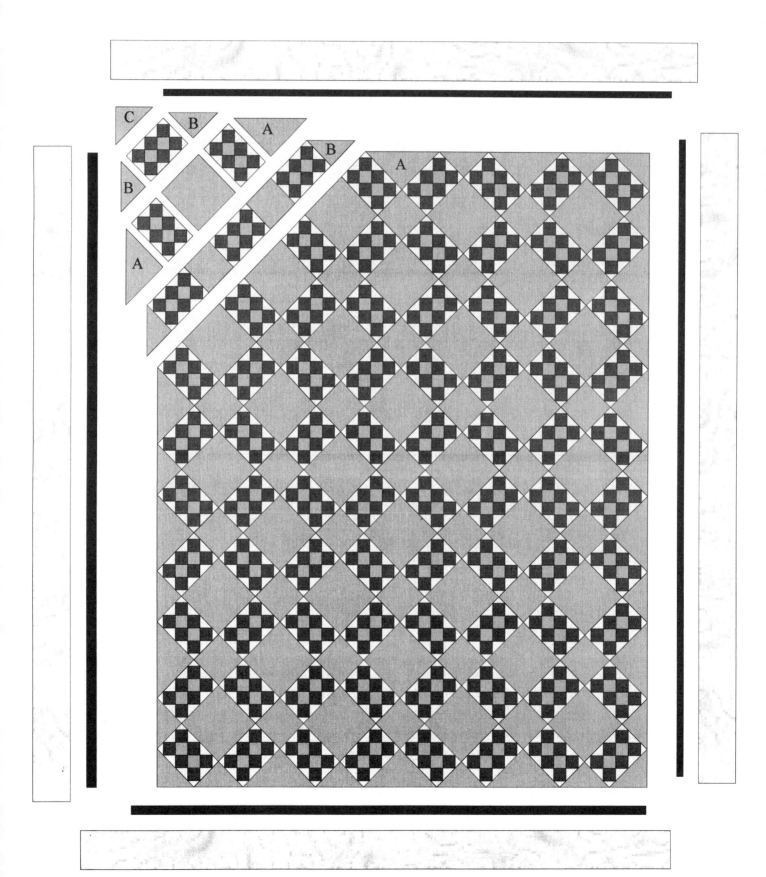

Red Cross Postage Stamp

Lap Size Quilt Diagramed

Photo found inside front cover.

Fabric Requirements

	Lap	Double	Queen
	67 1/2" x 79 1/2"	79 1/2" x 91 1/2"	91 1/2" x 103 1/2"
	30 10 1/2" blocks	42 10 1/2" blocks	56 10 1/2" blocks
Assorted '30s Prints	4 yards	5 yards	6 3/4 yards
Indigo Prints	2 3/8 yards	3 1/8 yards	3 3/4 yards
Solid Red "Cross"	1 1/4 yards	1 1/2 yards	2 1/4 yards
Solid Blue Center Square	1/4 yard	1/4 yard	3/4 yard
Backing	4 1/4 yards	5 1/2 yards	8 1/4 yards
Binding	3/4 yard	3/4 yard	1 yard

Cutting Instructions

		Lap	Double	Queen
Assorted '30s Prints	2" strips	65 strips	83 strips	112 strips
Indigo	2" strips	38 strips	49 strips	60 strips
Solid Red	2" strips	18 strips	21 strips	34 strips
Solid Blue	2" strips	2 strips	2 strips	3 strips
Binding - 2 1/2" strips		8 strips	9 strips	10 strips

Strip Assembly

1. Strip set 1 - Stitch seven 2" strips of assorted '30s prints together as diagramed at right. Press the seams in one direction. Resulting strip should measure 11" wide. Subcut the strips into 2" units.

	Lap	Double	Queen
Construct	3	4	5 1/2
Subcut Units	60	84	112

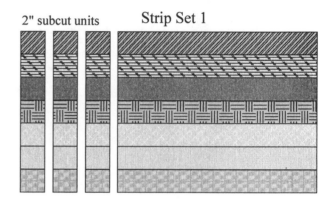

2" subcut units   Strip Set 1

2. Strip set 2 - Stitch six 2" strips of assorted '30s fabrics together as diagramed with a red 2" strip in the center. Press the seams in one direction. Resulting strip should measure 11" wide. Subcut the strips into 2" units.

	Lap	Double	Queen
Construct	3	4	5 1/2
Subcut Units	60	84	112

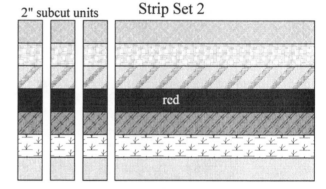

2" subcut units   Strip Set 2

3. Strip set 3 - Stitch four 2" strips of assorted '30s fabrics together with three 2" red strips in the center. Press the seams in one direction. Resulting strip should measure 11" wide. Subcut the strips into 2" units.

	Lap	Double	Queen
Construct	3	4	5 1/2
Subcut Units	60	84	112

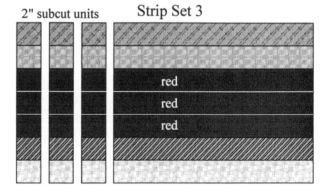

2" subcut units   Strip Set 3

4. Strip set 4 - Stitch two 2" strips of assorted '30s fabrics, four 2" red strips and a 2" blue strip in the center. Press the seams in one direction. Resulting strip should measure 11" wide. Subcut the strips into 2" units.

	Lap	Double	Queen
Construct	1 1/2	2	3
Subcut Units	30	42	56

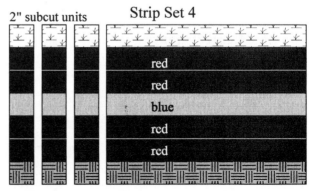

2" subcut units   Strip Set 4

5. Strip set 5 - Indigo Sashing - Stitch seven 2" strips of assorted indigo prints together as diagramed at right. Press the seams in one direction. Resulting strip should measure 11" wide. Subcut the strips into 2" units.

	Lap	Double	Queen
Construct	4	5	6 1/4
Subcut Units	71	97	127

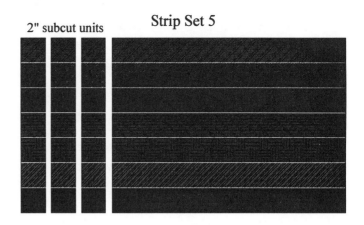

2" subcut units   Strip Set 5

6. Pieced Border Strip Set - Stitch assorted 2" strips of '30s fabrics to 2" strips of indigo prints. Press the seams toward the indigo prints. Subcut the strips into 2" units.

	Lap	Double	Queen
Construct	9	11	12
Subcut Units	188	220	252

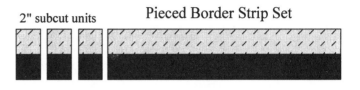

2" subcut units   Pieced Border Strip Set

7. Posts - Cut 2" wide strips of indigo print fabric into 2" squares for the posts.

	Lap	Double	Queen
Strips	2	3	4
2"Squares	42	56	72

2" squares   Posts

Block Construction

Assemble the blocks as diagramed below. The arrows indicate the direction of the pressed seams - allowing all seams to oppose. Press the long block seams in one direction.

	Lap	Double	Queen
Make	30	42	56

Pieced Border Construction

Stitch the 2" units from step #6 at left into chains, alternating the indigo squares. Press all seams in one direction. Construct 2 side border strips and 2 top/bottom strips following the unit count below.

	Lap	Double	Queen
Side Borders	49 units	57 units	65 units
Top/Bottom	45 units	53 units	61 units

→ Strip Set 1
← Strip Set 2
→ Strip Set 3
← Strip Set 4
→ Strip Set 3
← Strip Set 2
→ Strip Set 1

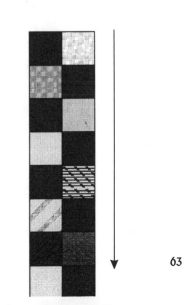

Quilt Top Assembly

1. Join blocks and sashing strips together into rows: lap - 5 x 6, double - 6 x 7, and queen - 7 x 8. Place all long block seams in a horizontal position, with these seams pressed down. Position the pieced sashing strips to create opposing seams. Press all seams in one direction as indicated by arrow.

2. Join sashing/post units together into rows. Add a single post to the end of each row. Press all seams in one direction as indicated by arrow

.

3. Assemble rows of blocks with rows of sashing between them. Press the long seams toward the upper edge of the quilt. (All horizontal seams will be pressed toward the top of the quilt.)

4. Final Borders - Attach pieced side borders first and then the top and bottom borders. Press all seams toward the final border.

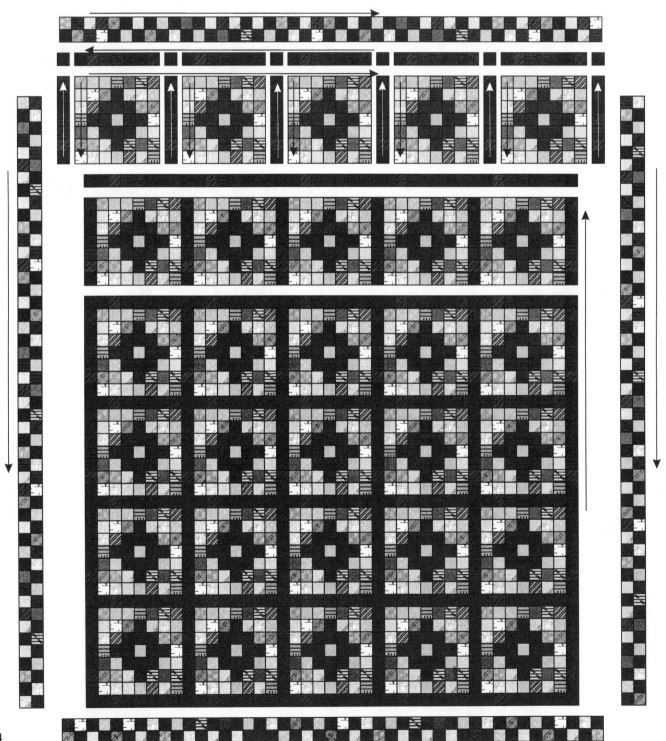

Amish Pinwheel

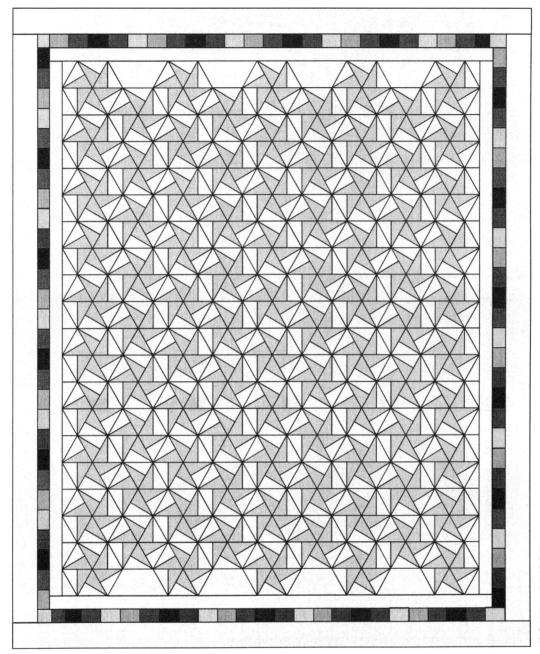

Double
Size Quilt
Diagramed

Photo found
on inside
back cover.

Fabric Requirements

	Lap	Double	Queen
	66" x 72"	80" x 96"	90" x 102"
	46 hexagons	86 hexagons	163 hexagons
Background	2 3/4 yards	4 3/8 yards	6 3/8 yards
Assorted Fabrics - Pinwheels	2 yards	3 3/8 yards	5 3/4 yards
Final Border	2 yards	2 3/4 yards	No Borders
Backing	4 1/4 yards	6 yards	8 1/2 yards
Binding	3/4 yard	3/4 yard	1 yard

Cutting Instructions

Background	Lap	Double	Queen
3 1/2" strips	16 strips	29 strips	54 strips
4 1/2" strips - Setting Triangles	3 strips	4 strips	6 strips
2 1/2" strips - First Border	6 strips	8 strips	No Borders
Assorted Colors			
3 1/2" strips	16 strips	29 strips	54 strips
3 1/2" strips - Pieced Border	6 strips	7 strips	No Borders
Final Border - sides	2 - 6 1/2" x 60"	2 - 6 1/2" x 84"	No Borders
- top and bottom	2 - 6 1/2" x 70"	2 - 6 1/2" x 85"	No Borders
Binding			
2 1/2" strips	7 strips	9 strips	10 strips

Hexagon Construction

1. Stitch each colored strip to a background strip along the long edge. Press the seam toward the colored fabric strip.

2. Stitch 4 strip pairs together. Press the seams toward the colored fabric strips. Straighten the strip end and subcut the sewn strips into 4 1/2" segments. Each 42" length should yield 9 units.

4 1/2" subcut units

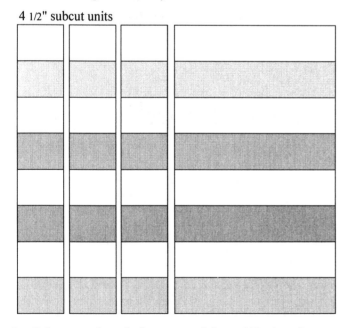

3. Subcut each unit from step 3 into 60° triangles using the **60° Clearview Triangle Ruler**. Place the 4 3/4" marking of the ruler at the lower edge of your strip. The center marking of the ruler will be on the seam. The colored fabric will be to the left of the center line, and the background fabric at the right of the center line. The tip of the ruler will be off the edge of your fabric. **Trim off the excess at the left of the ruler and set aside to be used in step 5.** Then cut along the right edge of the ruler. You may cut the strip using the **Template** on page 69 if the ruler is not available in your area.

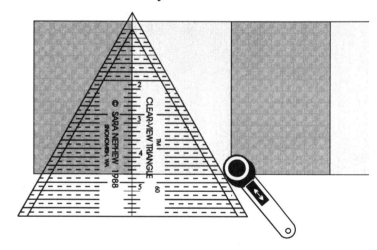

4. Rotate the ruler and again cut a triangle. Continue cutting triangles from the subcut strip of fabric.

Reserve "waste" triangle →

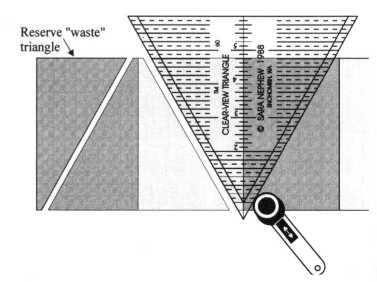

5. As you approach the end of the strip, sew the "waste" triangle cut in step 3 to the square end of the strip. Press the seam toward the background fabric. Reattaching the triangle will give one additional 60° triangle unit. Each strip will yield 8 60° triangle units.

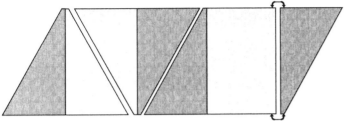

6. Stitch two identical triangles together as diagramed below. Press the seam toward the dark fabric. Repeat with a second pair of triangles.

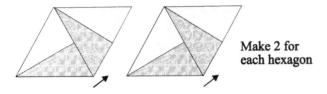

Make 2 for each hexagon

7. Add the third triangle. Press the seam toward the dark fabric. This will give you two identical half hexagons. Leave these in half hexagon form. The quilt top will be assembled in rows of half hexagons.

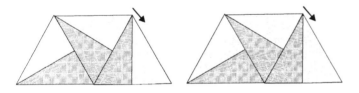

8. Repeat steps 6 and 7 using all triangles.

Make:
Lap	92 half hexagons
Double	172 half hexagons
Queen	326 half hexagons

Setting Triangles

Place the 4 1/2" wide strips of background fabric on the cutting mat folded, **wrong sides together.** This will allow you to cut Template I and Template I reversed at one time. Cut the strips into the number of units listed below using **Template I, I-r** and **Template J** located on page 69.

	Lap	Double	Queen
Template I	14	20	26
Template I-r	14	20	26
Template J	6	8	12

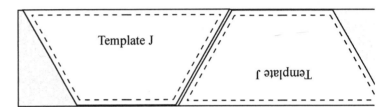

Folded strip of fabric used to produce Template I and I-r.

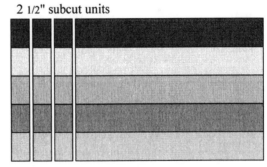

Piece First Border

1. Order the 3 1/2" wide cut strips of border fabric into a pleasing color arrangement. Stitch the strips together in pairs, and then into a larger strata. Press all seams in one direction.

2. Straighten the strip end. Cut the strip unit into 2 1/2" wide segments.

2 1/2" subcut units

3. Stitch the 2 1/2" segments together into a long chain. Trim the strip to the lengths necessary to border your quilt.

Quilt Top Assembly

1. Arrange the half hexagons on your floor or design wall.

2. Study the quilt pictured in the quilt gallery. Rearrange the hexagons until you find an arrangement that pleases you. It may be helpful to use an instant camera to photograph your work in progress so that you do not lose your favorite arrangement in the shuffle.

3. Stitch the half hexagons together into rows, beginning and ending each row with a Template I or I-r piece. Then stitch the rows together, carefully matching the seams.

4. Diagonally piece the first border strips together, cut lengths as needed. Apply the side borders first and then the top and bottom borders. Press the seams toward the border strips. (**The queen size quilt does not receive any borders.**)

5. Trim the pieced border strips to length as needed. Apply the side borders first and then the top and bottom borders. Press the seams toward the first border.

6. Trim final borders to fit and apply to the quilt top, attach side borders first, and then the top and bottom borders. Press all seams toward the border strips.

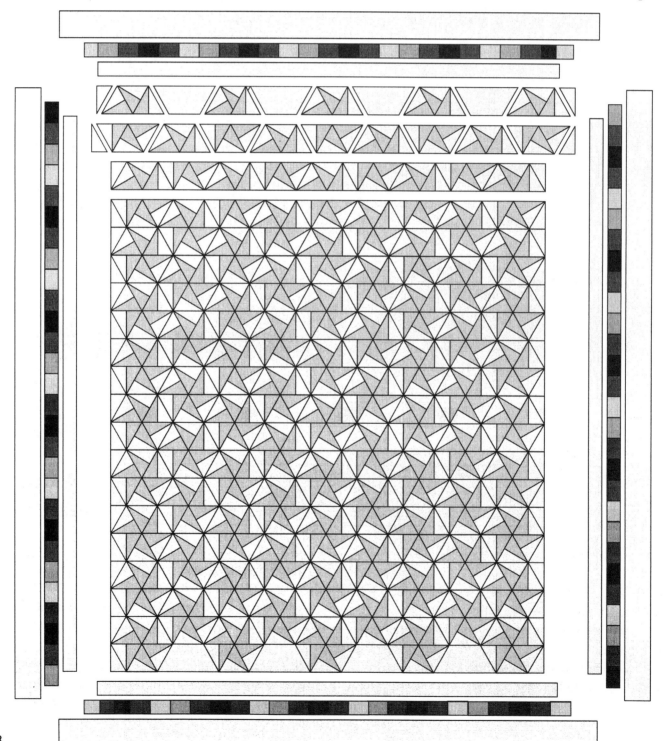

Lap and Queen Quilt Assembly

The lap and queen quilt top assembly differ only in the number of hexagons arranged.

Lap - 4 complete hexagons across the top
7 complete hexagons along the side

Queen -7 complete hexagons across the top
13 complete hexagons along the side

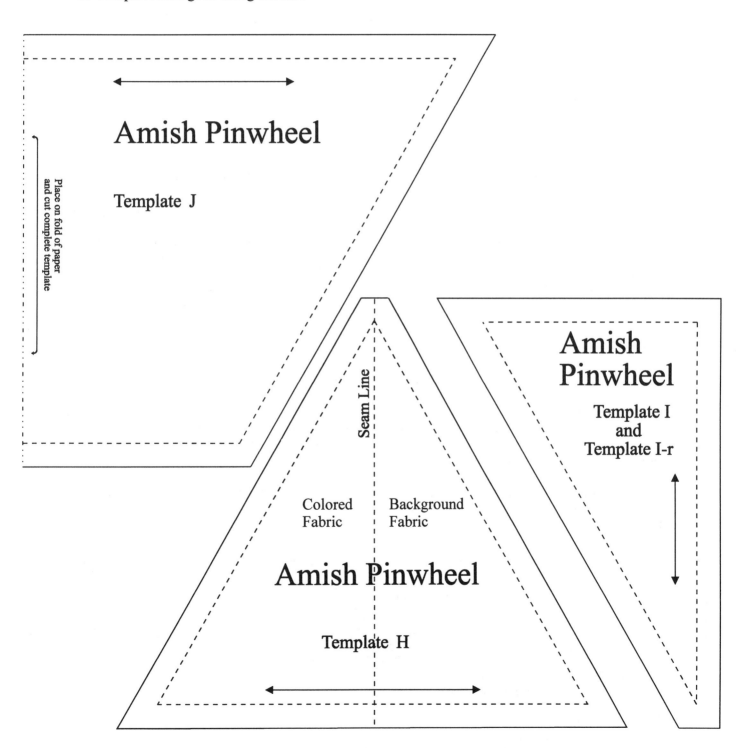

Amish Pinwheel

Template J

Place on fold of paper and cut complete template

Amish Pinwheel

Template I
and
Template I-r

Seam Line

Colored Fabric | Background Fabric

Amish Pinwheel

Template H

Quilter's Cheat Sheet

Half Square Triangles

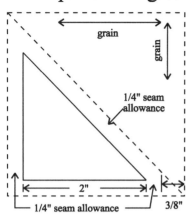

Finished Size + 7/8" = Cut Square

Quarter Square Triangles

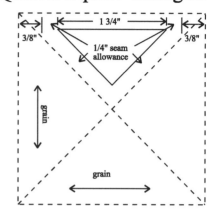

Finished Size + 1 1/4" = Cut Square

Corner Triangles

A diagonal set quilt requires a half square triangle at each corner to complete the quilt top.

A = the known block measurement
B = the unknown measurement

$A \div 1.414 = B$
$B + 7/8" =$ Cut size of square
Each square will yield 2 triangles.

Setting Triangles

A diagonal set quilt requires quarter square triangles to fill in the gaps along the sides of the quilt top.

A = the known block measurement
B = the unknown measurement

$A \times 1.414 = B$
$B + 1 1/4" =$ Cut size of square
Cut square will yield four triangles.

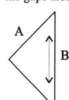

Bias Binding

Bias binding is a must for quilts with curved edges, and a longer wearing treatment for bed quilts. Crossgrain binding has a single thread that runs the length of the outermost edge of the quilt. A worn spot can easily open up the length of the quilt. With a bias binding, the threads run across the edge diagonally. One weak thread can cause only local damage.
Yardage requirements are the same for crossgrain bindings and bias bindings.

Cut a single layer of yardage at a 45° angle. Stitch selvages together using a 1" wide seam. Trim selvages to 1/4" and press the seam open. Cut yardage into bias strips 2 1/2" wide. Stitch the strip ends together. Press the seams open. Fold bias strip in half, wrong side together. Bind the quilt in the usual fashion.

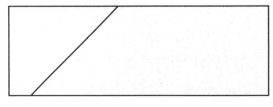

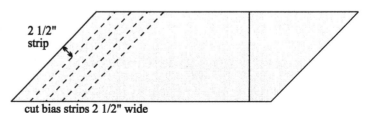

2 1/2" strip

cut bias strips 2 1/2" wide

Stitch the diagonal ends together using a 1/4" seam allowance.

Standard Sizes

	Mattress	Batting	Quilt
Crib	23" x 46"	45" x 60"	37" x 52" - 56"
Twin	39" x 75"	72" x 90"	70" x 90" - 96"
Double	54" x 75"	81" x 96"	80" x 90" - 96"
Queen	60" x 80"	90" x 108"	90" x 96" - 100"
King	76" x 80"	120" x 120"	104" x 96" - 100"

Mattress size + desired drop = quilt size. *Drop* is the portion of the quilt that falls below the edge of the mattress. Consider the usage of the quilt when determining the drop.

Backing Yardages

Backing should be 6" to 8" larger than the completed quilt top. Yardage is figured on 43" of usable fabric width after shrinkage and selvage elimination. Measure the quilt top to determine the length and the width.

Single Length
Widths up to 37" = length + 6"

Two Lengths
Widths 38" to 80" = (length x 2) + 12"
Remove the selvages and sew one lengthwise seam. Press to one side.

Three Widths
Widths greater than 80" = (width x 3) + 18"
Remove the selvages and sew two crosswise seams. Press to one side.

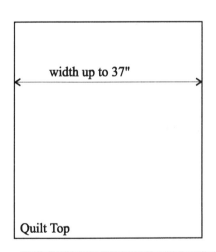

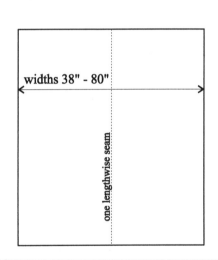

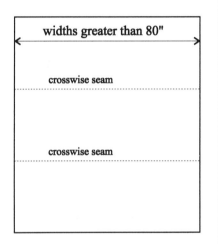

Mitered Binding

Stitch binding to the quilt edge. Start and stop the seam 1/4" from the quilt corner. Backtack at each end. Fold the strip away from the quilt top, and then down into position to stitch the second edge. Start and stop the seam 1/4" from the quilt corners. Continue in this manner around the quilt.

Draw lines **A**, **B**, and **C** as shown. Stitch on lines **B** and **C**. Trim excess and turn point right side out. Hand stitch fold in place.

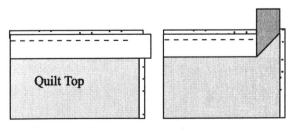

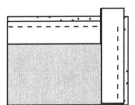

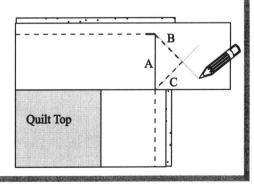

1 1/2" Quick Cut Cheat Sheet

34 1/2"	22 1/2"	10 1/2"
33"	21"	9"
31 1/2"	19 1/2"	7 1/2"
30"	18"	6"
28 1/2"	16 1/2"	4 1/2"
27"	15"	3"
25 1/2"	13 1/2"	1 1/2"
24"	12"	

1 3/4" Quick Cut Cheat Sheet

35"	17 1/2"
33 1/4"	15 3/4"
31 1/2"	14"
29 3/4"	12 1/4"
28"	10 1/2"
26 1/4"	8 3/4"
24 1/2"	7"
22 3/4"	5 1/4"
21"	3 1/2"
19 1/4"	1 3/4"

2" Quick Cut Cheat Sheet

34"	16"
32"	14"
30"	12"
28"	10"
26"	8"
24"	6"
22"	4"
20"	2"
18"	

2 1/2" Quick Cut Cheat Sheet

35"	17 1/2"
32 1/2"	15"
30"	12 1/2"
27 1/2"	10"
25"	7 1/2"
22 1/2"	5"
20"	2 1/2"